WENDY OLOGE

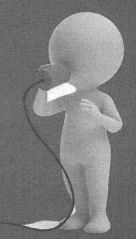

SOLVING
FAMILY PROBLEMS
THROUGH
EFFECTIVE COMMUNICATION

SOLVING FAMILY PROBLEMS THROUGH EFFECTIVE COMMUNICATION

TABLE OF CONTENTS

INTRODUCTION

When it comes to solving family problems through effective communication, you should ask yourself the following questions, "What can I do differently?" "How do I talk?"
Other things come into play when we talk about communication. Do you think, growing up you learned how to communicate effectively? Was there a system in your home? Did it give you the freedom to communicate effectively?

When I started the journey of effective communication, learning to communicate properly, I realized that it was a whole lot more than just speaking or expressing my views. Effective communication is not merely airing your views. You can air your views and still not communicate effectively.

Most of the families we have today are either transactional, superficial, or at most functional. Many families are more transactional than others. Most people rarely build transformational families and that's why you are holding this book in your hands because solving family problems through effective communication can only happen if you are building a transformational family.

Communication is a basic building block for our relationships. Through communication, we convey our thoughts, feelings, and connections to one another, so communication is the biggest deal in every family.
We got married about 15 years ago and one of the gaps that we saw was communication. We sat down and said to ourselves, "If we do not learn how to communicate effectively our relationship is going to die with time. It's going to play out like every other relationship that we see around us". It's interesting because that's all we see. My husband and I decided we would make communication a big deal, so we started taking communication classes every year.
Today, it is interesting how communication goes in my home. When there is a problem, we can easily slide it through. We disagree

sometimes, but we are more interested in being one than we are, in being right, which is a key aspect. We all have our experiences where we feel misunderstood and even ignored. Believe me, when we are less angry and less stressed, we are more open to resolving problems than when we feel misunderstood.

I like the scriptures a lot. James 1:19 says: *"Know these my beloved brothers; let every person be quick to hear, slow to speak, and slow to anger."*

I will leave you with this thought, while we go on with this conversation.

A Note From Me To You

In a world where the dynamics of family life are ever-evolving, effective communication stands as the cornerstone of harmonious relationships within our homes. As a passionate advocate for intentional parenting, I, Wendy Ologe, founder of the Intentional Parent Academy and author of several books on parenting, wholeheartedly understand the pivotal role that communication plays in the life of every family.

My journey in the realm of parenting and family dynamics has led me to witness both the immense joys and the profound challenges that come with this territory. Throughout my years of research, interviews, and personal experiences, it has become undeniably clear that effective communication is the bedrock upon which the structure of a healthy family is built. It is the key to resolving conflicts, fostering understanding, and nurturing the love that binds us together.

As parents, we embark on a lifelong voyage of guiding our children, and in doing so, we encounter a myriad of issues, concerns, and complexities. Whether you are a seasoned parent seeking to navigate the treacherous waters of teenage rebellion or a new parent striving to build the strongest foundation for your growing family, this book, "Solving Family Problems Through Effective Communication", aims to be your trusted companion.

Throughout the pages of this book, we will explore the multifaceted nature of family dynamics and the art of communication within the family unit. We will delve into the barriers that often hinder effective communication, unravel the various communication styles, and discover the transformative power of active listening and non-verbal cues.

Furthermore, we will equip you with a toolbox of effective communication strategies, tools, and techniques that will empower you to navigate the challenges and triumphs that life within a family brings. Whether it's addressing sibling rivalries, improving parent-child communication, or tackling the unique dynamics of blended or extended families, you will find guidance tailored to your specific needs.

Our modern world is heavily influenced by technology, and we will also explore its role in family communication, both the positive and the negative aspects. Finding a balance between the screen-dominated world and the need for face-to-face connection is a crucial challenge for today's families, and we will offer insights to help you navigate this terrain.

In our journey, we will also consider the impact of culture on family communication. Recognizing and respecting cultural differences can lead to a richer and more inclusive family environment, embracing the unique qualities each family member brings to the table.

When challenges become overwhelming, we will discuss the prospect of seeking professional help. Family therapy or counselling can provide an essential lifeline in times of crisis, and we'll guide you on how to make this decision and find the right therapist for your family's needs.

At the heart of it all, this book is not just about theory; it is a practical guide to nurturing positive communication habits within your family. You will learn how to create a safe space for family discussions, set boundaries, and manage emotions, ultimately building a stronger and more resilient family unit.

With a roadmap to healthier family dynamics in hand, we invite you to embark on a journey of healing, understanding, and growth. This book is designed to be your compass, helping you navigate the sometimes turbulent seas of family life, steering you towards stronger connections, and ultimately, towards the fulfilment of the ultimate goal: healing hearts.

Join me on this voyage through the pages of "Solving Family Problems Through Effective Communication", and let us explore the transformative power of communication within your family. Together, we will set sail toward a brighter, more harmonious family future.

CHAPTER 1
UNDERSTANDING FAMILY DYNAMICS

Family dynamics are like the intricate and ever-changing patterns of a kaleidoscope, creating a unique and beautiful picture that is your family.

One of the major reasons family relationships break down is because of the lack of connection, communication, and contributions. Unfortunately, most of our communications are full of counsel, condemnation, and criticism but never with connection, conversation, or contribution.

LACK OF CONNECTION

Emotional Distance: Many families experience emotional distance among their members. This can be due to a range of reasons, including busy schedules, differing interests, unresolved conflicts, or generational gaps. When family members feel emotionally disconnected, it can erode the sense of belonging and closeness that should exist within a family.

Technological Distraction: In the digital age, technological distractions have become a significant barrier to emotional connection. Family members may spend more time engrossed in screens than interacting with each other. This can result in physical presence but emotional absence, contributing to feelings of isolation.

COMMUNICATION ISSUES

Negative Communication Patterns: Families can develop negative communication patterns over time. These patterns may involve criticism, blame, or condemnation. When negative communication becomes the norm, it creates an unhealthy environment. Instead of feeling supported and heard, family members can end up feeling attacked and become defensive.

Lack of Constructive Feedback: In some families, constructive feedback may be lacking. Instead of offering feedback that helps each other grow, family members may focus on pointing out flaws and mistakes. This can lead to a defensive attitude and make it difficult for individuals to accept feedback or discuss concerns openly.

CONTRIBUTIONS AND RESPONSIBILITIES

Sharing Responsibilities: Family life involves various responsibilities, including household chores, financial contributions, and emotional support. When one or more family members fail to contribute their fair share, it can create feelings of imbalance and resentment. This lack of contribution can extend to both tangible and emotional aspects of family life.

Communication Gaps: Sometimes, family members may not effectively communicate about responsibilities and contributions. Misunderstandings and assumptions can result in unequal burdens. This can lead to frustration, as some people may feel overworked, while others may feel disconnected from the family's functioning.
Fostering connection, communication, and contributions in family life is an ongoing and evolving process. It demands patience, empathy, and a commitment to nurturing the bonds between family members.

By addressing these issues head-on, families can work towards stronger, healthier, and more harmonious relationships.

To truly navigate the challenges and triumphs within your family, it's important to know these dynamics thoroughly. There are various facets of family dynamics and they manifest in real-life scenarios. Let's go on a journey together where I will draw from my experiences and other relatable examples that might resonate with your own family.

TYPES OF FAMILY STRUCTURES

Families come in all shapes and sizes. While the traditional nuclear family, consisting of two parents and their biological children, remains a common model, families today exhibit an array of structures. For instance, the growing number of single-parent families. In my circle, my friend has been raising her two children on her own for several years after she lost her husband some 10 years ago. Understanding how the absence of one parent influences the family's dynamics, particularly in decision-making and support systems, is a significant aspect of comprehending family structures.

The Traditional Nuclear Family: This is the family model many of us grew up with, consisting of two parents (a mother and a father) and their biological children. In this structure, roles are often clearly defined. For instance, the father might be the primary breadwinner while the mother manages the household. This structure can provide a sense of stability, but it may also place unique pressures on parents to conform to societal expectations. My parents followed this model, which sometimes led to traditional gender roles and expectations that we all had to navigate.

Single-Parent Families: In single-parent families, one parent takes on the role of both caregiver and provider. My friend's family, for instance, falls into this category. She became a single parent after her divorce and had to juggle the responsibilities of parenting, earning a living, and maintaining the household. Single-parent families can be incredibly resilient, but they may face challenges in providing emotional support, financial stability, and quality time due to a single adult's limited resources.

Blended Families: Blended families emerge when parents remarry, bringing their children from previous marriages into a new family structure. The interactions between step-siblings, step-parents, and biological children can create complex dynamics. I have a few parents in our inner circle program who run this model of a family. Negotiating the roles and relationships within their family unit has been an ongoing journey, marked by moments of joy, adjustment, and sometimes conflict. Understanding the intricate dynamics of blended families is crucial for promoting harmony and unity.

Extended Families: Extended families encompass not only parents and children but also a wider network of relatives, such as grandparents, aunts, uncles, and cousins, all living under the same roof or nearby. This structure is common in many cultures and can be a source of emotional support, shared responsibilities, and a rich family culture. However, it may also present challenges related to privacy, decision-making, and potential conflicts. In my family, we often gathered for holidays and special occasions, involving multiple generations and diverse personalities. This dynamic led to cherished traditions but also the need for careful management of differences and expectations.

By examining these family structures and reflecting on your own experiences, you can better appreciate the nuances of your family dynamics. Each structure has its unique strengths and challenges, and understanding them allows you to navigate family life with greater empathy, flexibility, and adaptability. As we delve further into family dynamics, these insights will serve as a foundation for addressing the common issues and improving communication within your family.

HOW FAMILY DYNAMICS AFFECT COMMUNICATION

Family dynamics and communication are intrinsically linked, as the way a family operates directly influences how its members interact and communicate with one another. Understanding how family dynamics affect communication is vital for addressing and improving the quality of these interactions. Here are some key ways in which family dynamics impact communication:

Power Dynamics: In many families, power dynamics play a significant role in communication. This can manifest in different ways, such as a parent-child hierarchy, where parents hold more authority, or even in sibling rivalries, where power struggles can occur. These dynamics affect how family members express themselves, as those with less perceived power might hesitate to voice their opinions or concerns. Clear recognition of these dynamics is essential to ensure that all family members have a voice and are heard.

Communication Patterns: Every family develops its unique communication patterns over time. Some families are openly expressive, encouraging open dialogue and emotional sharing, while others may be more reserved or prone to bottling up feelings. For instance, in a family where emotions are seldom expressed, a child might grow up believing that sharing feelings is discouraged, leading to challenges in expressing emotions later in life. Recognizing these patterns and their impact on communication is crucial for fostering a healthier communication environment.

Roles and Expectations: Family roles and expectations can dictate communication styles. For example, in a traditional family, gender roles may influence how men and women express themselves. A father may be expected to exhibit strength and stoicism, while a mother is expected to be nurturing and empathetic. These predefined roles can lead to suppressed emotions and hinder open communication. It's important to challenge and redefine these roles to create a more open and inclusive communication environment.

Past Baggage and Grudges: Family dynamics can be shaped by past conflicts, unresolved issues, and emotional baggage. When family members carry unresolved grudges or hurt, it can create a climate of tension and resentment that hampers effective communication. For instance, if two siblings had a significant fall-out in their youth and never addressed the issue, they may struggle to communicate as adults, always tiptoeing around the unresolved conflict. Acknowledging and addressing past baggage is essential for creating a more open and honest dialogue.

Family Culture and Traditions: Every family has its unique culture and traditions that influence communication. Whether it's a cultural emphasis on respect for elders, a tradition of weekly family meetings, or a habit of discussing important matters only during holidays, these customs can either facilitate or hinder effective communication. Being mindful of these traditions and their impact on communication can help adapt them to better suit the family's evolving needs.

Changes in Family Structure: Transitions and changes within the family, such as the birth of a new child, the loss of a family member, or a parent's divorce, relocation can significantly affect family dynamics and, in turn, communication. These changes can disrupt established communication patterns and may require a period of adjustment to accommodate the evolving family structure.

Understanding the interplay between family dynamics and communication is a critical step toward fostering a healthier and more productive family environment. By acknowledging the impact of power dynamics, communication patterns, roles and expectations, past baggage, family culture, and changes in family structure, family members can work together to adapt and enhance their communication, leading to more harmonious and fulfilling relationships.

BARRIERS TO EFFECTIVE COMMUNICATION IN FAMILIES

Effective communication within families is essential for building strong relationships and resolving conflicts. However, several barriers can hinder this process. Let's delve deeper into each of the subheadings to explore how these barriers manifest in family settings and how they can be addressed.

a. Lack of Active Listening

Effective communication involves not only speaking but also active listening. In families, the failure to listen attentively can lead to misunderstandings, miscommunications, and strained relationships. Here's how this barrier can manifest:

- Selective Listening: Family members may hear what is being said, but they only pay attention to parts that interest them or fit their preconceived notions. For instance, a teenager might listen to the part of the parent's lecture about curfew but tune out the reasoning behind it.
- Interrupting: Frequent interruptions during conversations can hinder the speaker's ability to convey their message. This might happen when one family member is eager to share their opinion or assert their point of view. For example, when discussing vacation plans, a family member might interrupt someone who is describing their preferred destination.

Addressing the Lack of Active Listening: Encouraging active listening in the family can be achieved by setting ground rules for conversations, such as taking turns to speak without interruptions. Family members can also practice reflective listening, where they repeat what they've heard to ensure they understand each other.

b. Misunderstandings and Misinterpretations

Misunderstandings and misinterpretations are common barriers to effective family communication. These can arise from differences in communication styles, language barriers, or varying interpretations of gestures and tone. In family interactions, they might manifest in the following ways:

- Assumptions: Family members may assume they know what another person means without seeking clarification. For instance, if a parent tells their child to "clean up," the child may interpret it as cleaning their room, while the parent meant tidying up the entire house.
- Non-Verbal Misinterpretations: Tone of voice, facial expressions, and body language play a significant role in communication. Misinterpretations can occur when family members read into non-verbal cues that were not intended. For instance, a sigh from a spouse might be interpreted as annoyance when it could have been a sign of tiredness.

Addressing Misunderstandings and Misinterpretations: Clear and open communication is key to addressing these barriers. Encouraging family members to ask for clarification when they are unsure about something can prevent misunderstandings. Families can also practice active listening and confirm their understanding by summarizing what was said.

c. Emotional Baggage

Emotional baggage refers to unresolved emotional issues from the past that family members carry with them. These unresolved feelings can affect current interactions and communication. Some ways in which emotional baggage can affect family communication include:

- Resentment: Past conflicts or grievances that have not been properly addressed can lead to lingering resentment, which can resurface in current interactions.
- Avoidance: Family members may avoid certain topics or discussions because they fear reigniting old wounds. This avoidance can hinder open and honest communication.

Addressing Emotional Baggage: Addressing emotional baggage often requires open and empathetic communication. Families can benefit from setting aside time to discuss past conflicts, express their feelings, and work toward resolution. Counselling or therapy may also help deal with deep-seated emotional issues.

d. Avoidance and Denial

In some families, members may avoid addressing difficult issues or deny that problems exist. This barrier to effective communication can manifest in the following ways:

Silent Treatment: Family members may give each other the silent treatment when conflicts arise, refusing to communicate altogether.

Denial of Problems: Some families may deny the existence of issues, choosing to ignore or downplay them. For example, a family dealing with addiction may pretend that the problem does not exist.

Addressing Avoidance and Denial: Overcoming avoidance and denial requires fostering an environment of trust and open communication. Family members should feel safe discussing problems without fear of judgment or retaliation. Encouraging family meetings where concerns can be raised and addressed is one approach to breaking down these barriers.

Addressing these barriers to effective communication in families involves awareness, willingness to change, and a commitment to open, honest, and empathetic interactions. By recognizing and actively working to overcome these barriers, families can build stronger, more supportive relationships.

CHAPTER 2

COMMUNICATION STYLES IN FAMILIES

A father shared with me the experience of punishing his son whom he said kept disobeying him by constantly going around the corner. Each time he did so, the father would yell and punish him and tell him not to go around the corner again but the little boy kept doing it. Finally, after one day of such punishment, the boy looked the father in the eyes and said "What does corner mean Daddy?"

Most of the problems we have with our children, spouse, and siblings are usually a lack of effective communication. Most of us were conditioned with the wrong kind of communication. The Governor and I had to take communication classes yearly because we realized that if we would build a better home than what we see around us, then effective communication must be learned.

People Don't see the world as it is, they see it as they are or as they have been conditioned to be.

At the heart of every family's pain is misunderstanding.

There is no way to have rich rewarding family relationships without real understanding. Most of our family relationships are superficial, transactional, and at most functional but you can build a transformational family relationship.

Within a family, various communication styles can influence how members interact and relate to one another. These styles are shaped by individual personalities, upbringing, and the family's unique dynamics. Understanding the different communication styles in families is essential for improving family relationships and resolving conflicts. Here, we explore common communication styles and how they manifest in family settings:

PASSIVE COMMUNICATION

Passive communication is characterized by an avoidance of conflict and a reluctance to express one's own needs and opinions. In a family with passive communicators, you might observe:

- **Unspoken Resentment**
Family members may harbour unexpressed feelings of frustration or resentment, which can simmer beneath the surface, creating tension.

- **Lack of Self-Advocacy**
Family members who employ passive communication often struggle to assert themselves or express their needs, leading to unmet expectations and dissatisfaction.

- **Avoidance of Difficult Topics**
Sensitive or challenging topics are frequently avoided, leading to unresolved issues and unaddressed concerns.

Impact: Passive communication can lead to misunderstandings, emotional distance, and unresolved conflicts within the family.

AGGRESSIVE COMMUNICATION

Aggressive communication is characterized by a domineering and confrontational approach to interactions. In families with aggressive communicators, you might notice:

- **Blame and Accusations**
Aggressive family members may engage in blaming and accusing, often pointing fingers rather than seeking solutions.

- **Verbal or Emotional Attacks**
Arguments can escalate into verbal or emotional attacks, leaving family members feeling hurt and defensive.

- **Dominance**
Aggressive communicators often seek to dominate conversations and decision-making, which can lead to feelings of powerlessness in other family members.

Impact: Aggressive communication can create a hostile and fearful family environment, where open and honest dialogue becomes challenging.

ASSERTIVE COMMUNICATION

Assertive communication strikes a balance between passive and aggressive styles. In families where assertive communication prevails, you'll observe:

- **Clear Expression of Needs**

Family members are comfortable expressing their needs and preferences while respecting the needs of others.

- **Open Dialogue**
Conversations are characterized by active listening and a willingness to engage in problem-solving and compromise.

- **Healthy Conflict Resolution**
Conflicts are approached as opportunities for growth and understanding, rather than as battles to be won.

Impact: Assertive communication fosters trust, mutual respect, and the resolution of conflicts within the family, leading to healthier relationships.

PASSIVE-AGGRESSIVE COMMUNICATION

Passive-aggressive communication combines elements of both passive and aggressive styles. In families with passive-aggressive communicators, you might observe:

- **Indirect Expressions of Displeasure**
Family members may express dissatisfaction or anger indirectly, often through sarcasm, backhanded compliments, or passive resistance.

- **Subtle Acts of Sabotage**
Passive-aggressive individuals may engage in subtle acts of resistance or sabotage to express their discontent.

- **Veiled Criticism**
Rather than directly addressing concerns, passive-aggressive communicators may resort to veiled criticism, leaving the recipient uncertain of their true intentions.

Impact: Passive-aggressive communication can lead to confusion, strained relationships, and unresolved conflicts within the family.

Understanding the prevalent communication styles within your family is the first step toward improving interactions and building healthier relationships. By recognizing these styles and their impacts, family members can work together to cultivate more assertive and open communication, fostering an environment of understanding and mutual respect.

WAYS TO IMPROVE EFFECTIVE COMMUNICATION SKILLS

These are the points to note in developing effective communication skills which are critical for a successful relationship:

1. Effective Communication Builders

Communication builders are tools that allow us to build communication effectively. With these communication builders, you can learn how to become an effective communicator and improve your relationships with others. This simple coaching tool can be used every day of your life in your family. The goal is to help you avoid confrontations, and work more efficiently as a team by learning how to communicate effectively with others in your home and so on.

2. Build a circle of influence over a circle of concern

If you must solve family problems through effective communication, you must start with your side of the card. The circle of concern is made up of things that are outside your control but they are your concern. The essence of productivity and the use of this is for us to begin to live in what I call the circle of influence instead of your circle of concern.

One of the ways to make the difference clear in our mind is to look in terms of these concerns. A circle of influence is a smaller circle within the circle of concern that embraces the things that we can usually do something about.

A parent came to me and was talking about not parenting a young man right. His parents were going through a divorce and by the time he was 21, they were fully separated.
This young man felt a great sense of duty to fix it, he would say to his dad, "Why not just go to Mommy and say sorry?"
And then go to the mom and say, "Why not go to Daddy and say sorry?"

The Mom will say "No, we cannot."
He came to me when he was about to get married and he said "I feel the guilt of my parents getting separated and I think I would have done something. I think that I was part of the reason why they got separated and I wish they had stayed together."
I said to him, "You need to realize that your greatest responsibility as a son is to love each of your parents".
This was a case of circle of concern and circle of influence.
I also told him, "You need to decide what you want."
He said he wanted a better family, he wanted a family that was growing, a marriage different from what he saw growing up.

I've found out that when you have this kind of resolve, it gives you the sustaining power to swallow hard in difficult moments, to say something that will hurt feelings, to apologize, and to come back to it because you see something more important to you than just about the emotion of the moment.
Say to yourself, "I am interested in building a transformational family."
When you make that resolve, everything that happens in your family - between you and your children, between you and your spouse - whenever there's an issue, it becomes easy to resolve. You realize that there is something bigger than just the heat of the moment.
This young man said he made a resolve to always remember that "it is more important to be one than to be right". This was something I'd told him. I encouraged him to go with that mindset in his marriage.

The tiny victory that comes from winning the argument only causes greater separation which deprives you of deeper satisfaction in a marriage relationship. If you say you want a transformational family, when emotions come up, what is going to ring in your head is that 'we have a transformational family'.

This can be one of your greatest life lessons. When you are faced with a situation, when you want something different from what your spouse wants, when you want something different from what it is that your family members or your children want, one of the things that you can do is to step back, re-affirm the love and then be determined to do everything in your power not to be perfect (because I know that it is impossible to be perfect), but to keep working on it and keep trying. It takes a lot of effort.

This young man realized that his parent's marriage was a circle of concern but it was not in his circle of influence. He decided to be proactive, he met a professional and he realized that he could not fix their marriage but he could work on something better, so he began to focus on his circle of influence. He worked on loving and supporting both parents even when it was hard and that was it. He gained the courage to act based on principles rather than just reacting to his parents' emotional response. He also started to think about his future and his own marriage, he began to recognize the values he wanted in his own relationship with his future wife, and as a result, he was able to build his marriage with the vision of that relationship in mind.
The power of that Vision had carried him through the challenges and had given him the power to apologize and to do things a lot more differently.

There was another parent who decided that the behaviour of their daughter had deteriorated to the point that they felt allowing her to continue to live in the home would destroy the family. They wanted this child to just go, and the father was determined that when she came home that day, they were going to talk to the child. When they came to me and they said they had decided to take this child back to Nigeria, he said that's the decision they had made because it was going to make a mess of their family. This girl was in trouble. I told the father to sit down with her and make at least five different lists. I told him to write the changes that she should make for her to stay, and while he is writing, he can turn to the other side of the card that is blank and ask himself "How can I do things a little differently?"

When talking about a circle of concern, the first thing that we must talk about is the ability to choose your response.

When he was done writing on that card, they came back to me and said it was just a simple exercise, but when he turned to the side of the card where he wrote what he would agree to do if his daughter agreed to make those changes, he was in tears because he realized that his list was longer than the girl's list and he was so sober. He was in tears by the time he was done and when the girl came home, instead of sending her back, he decided that he was going to talk to her since he had also seen his side of the coin. He realized that his choices made all of the difference.

Think about the word 'responsible'. This is the ability to choose your response. When you focus on your circle of influence, it gets larger and you are also modeling to others through your example. Others may do the opposite out of reactive anger but if you are sincere and persistent, your example can eventually impact the spirit of everyone and they become more proactive. There is more responsibility in the family culture.

Interestingly, after that conversation, the young girl started to change. They did not bring her back to Nigeria anymore. Her father called me and said she had changed and I asked them, "What changed?"

You also change responsibility. That is one core aspect of actually thinking of your circle of influence instead of your circle of concern. The concern for that father was a daughter who was doing something wrong but the influence that he could make was effective communication, that is how solving family problems through effective communication works.

3. Listening to your own language

One of the best ways to tell if you are in your circle of influence is to listen to your language. If you are in your circle of concern, your language will be blaming, accusing, and reactive. If you want to solve a family problem and you want to solve it through effective communication, one of the things you must do is listen to your language. If you are in your circle of influence, your language will be proactive, it will reflect a focus on the things that you can do something about and if you are in your circle of influence you can create rules in your family that will enable your children to learn these things better and do things differently. If you look out for teachable moments, you can start modelling the kind of loving interaction that you want with your spouse. You can learn more about your parents' mistakes, seek to understand them, and do something differently.

I have heard quite a number of you say "My parents...", you are still in your circle of concern. We are not taking away what your parents did but you have not moved from your circle of concern to your circle of influence and until you do that, there is no improvement and you are going to be stuck.

EXERCISE: I want you to take this experiment, you might want to ask your spouse or someone else to participate with you and give you feedback.

Identify a family problem: Describe it to someone, using completely reactive terms, focus on your circle of concern, and remember what I said about the circle of concern. Now describe the same problems and convince that person that the problem is not your fault, blame the next person, and accuse the person. I want you to write it down on two pages, focus on your responsibility, and talk about what you can do in your circle of influence. For instance, if your children are always yelling, focus on talking to someone about how your children are always yelling and how it is their fault and all of the reactivities, keep it to one side, and then convince yourself that it's not your fault. Write on the other one and say yes my children are yelling but what can I do differently?

Write what you can do differently, now look at the difference in the two descriptions. Which one more closely resembles your normal habit pattern when talking about family problems? Until you identify your habit when it comes to communication, you can't communicate effectively. You need to be able to identify what your habit is and how to communicate your issues.

This is not just about communicating, but how you can use communication as a problem-solving tool. Unfortunately, poor communication habits are so common that many people who use them are not even aware that they do. This makes improving the ability to communicate an uphill battle. If you find that you are using reactive language, you can take immediate steps and replace it with proactive words and phrases. There is something called Neuro-linguistic Programming, how you think of a problem in your head is going to reflect in how you solve them. The very act of forcing yourself to use words will help you recognize habits of reactivity and begin to change them.
Teaching responsibility for language is another way that we can help our children learn to integrate effective communication.

Recently, a parent reached out to me and said she was trying to help their three-year-old to be more responsible with language so I said to her, "Whenever she says something you don't want her to say, tell her 'in our family, we don't say 'hate', 'shut up' or call people 'stupid'. Mention it, and let her internalize the language you have to replace the one you don't want. Be careful how you talk to people and you need to be responsible."

The parents went back and started to try this, every now and then they would remind their daughter "Don't call people names, try to be responsible with the way you talk".

One of those days, the parents chatted with me and said that she was just saying "I hate this movie", and the daughter said, "Don't say hate mom, you are responsible."

That was like a hit back. You can begin to think about the habits that you had when it comes to communication, where and how you speak about a problem is very important.

You can always change a habit. There is evidence that the preference for a thing that sounds familiar is a product of neurology. Many times the brain just wants something that sounds familiar, that is why you can't help but call your children names even though you know that your children should not be called names. Your brain can't delete it, so when those things come you will call your child names because somewhere in your brain, the preference for the familiar is a product of your neurology. The good news is, habits can be changed. That's why we say, that when you repeat patterns, it just continues in your head. The brain is very good with repeating patterns. However, when habits are rooted in our minds they are not destiny.

My communication habit is not my destiny. I can change it, I can choose my habits.

We know how everything works, every habit no matter how complex, is manageable. To modify a habit you must decide to change it. You must consciously accept the hard work of identifying the cues, the routines, and the rewards that drive the habits, and then find alternatives. You must know that you have control and self-consciousness, that's when you're able to use it. If you believe you can change your habit, then you can change it.

To be able to change habits, you have to identify the routine. Otherwise, you will not be able to make changes. For instance, if you want to stop taking soda and you have identified that every time you sit down in your room and you are tired, the next thing is that you're going to walk down to a shop and get a drink. If you want to change that habit, one of the things is not just to say I want to change this habit or I want to stop it, you have to change the routine. What is the routine? The routine is walking down to that shop. What can you do instead of going to the shop? You can walk to another place.

Changing habits is an intentional thing and how does it work when it comes to changing habits in your communication? Instead of saying something, replace it even when your head tells you no, that's not what you want to say intentionally, speak it.
The Bible says to speak the word only, speak it intentionally, and tell yourself that you want to say it even if it doesn't sound right. Tell your brain that it doesn't have to sound right in your head. You need to change the routine so you need to restructure your head.

THE EMOTIONAL BANK ACCOUNT

A very important thing to note is that there is an emotional bank account. The emotional bank account represents the quality of the relationship that you have with others. It's like a financial bank account that is why you make deposits proactively, doing things that build relationships. Unfortunately, one of the things that we do is that we don't build. We don't fund the emotional bank account so we usually don't have reserves. And when there is a family problem, everywhere explodes because, in the emotional bank account, there's nothing to withdraw from it. You then make withdrawals by reactively doing things and that decreases the level of trust.

At any time, the balance of trust in the account determines how well you can communicate and solve problems with another person. If you have a high balance in your emotional bank account, you can even make a mistake in a relationship and if you have an emotional result it will compensate. There are people that what they will do to offend another person, would not offend me because of the emotional bank account that they have with me but if your account is low or even overdrawn, there is no trust and there is no authentic communication.

It is like working on minefields, you will always be on guard, you have to measure every word, and even good intentions are misunderstood. If there is no real communication, and no ability to work together and solve problems, the harder you push, the more it becomes a problem.

One of the biggest problems in many family cultures is a reactive tendency to continue to make withdrawals instead of making deposits. If you're thinking about what kind of impact this kind of communication day in and day out has on the balance of your emotional bank account, let me paint a picture for you of how communication with your teenager likely goes:

Morning: You are giving instructions

Afternoon: You are correcting harshly

Evening: You are giving further instructions.

No matter what the situation is, there will always be a problem. You say "I have done everything for these children. I do everything and they don't consider it".

Ask yourself, "Is my presence making things worse or better for my child?"

There was a parent who came to me and said that his daughter didn't trust him and whenever he tried to resolve their differences, they seemed to make things worse. I realized that he was the problem and I told him that.

That is why I keep saying that "parenting is about you".

I told him, "Why not change yourself? Why not change your heart towards this girl? I know that this girl has done stupid things, she has done all the bad things but don't compete with her, be on her side."

The first thing he told me was "I will tell my daughter that I've learned something".

Do you know that as he focused on changing his feelings and actions rather than hers, he began to see this girl in an entirely new light, he began to appreciate her great deeds to be loved.

I often say that the angry one is the one who deserves to be loved.

As he continued to let the negative blows bounce off, there was an increasing strength, no longer inner resentment, he began to increase in his love for her almost without effort. He found himself beginning to do little things for her, little favours. One day, the girl looks at him and says, "Daddy there is something different about you, what is happening? What's going on?"

He responded, "I have just come to realize some things about myself and I need to change and I'm grateful that I can now express my love to you by treating you the way I know I should have treated you all along."

Parents, you need to stop doing parenting transactionally. All you do is "After I carried you for nine months", "I paid your school fees". It's always about transactions, you need to take it away. Sincerely and consistently make points if you are looking to solve any family problem, and as you do, you begin to see the person differently.

Replace self-serving motives with actual service motives. "I'm raising my children well" is a self-serving motive.

"I'm the coach, people should see my children as perfect because they validate me".

That's transactional, that is me asserting myself and that's not why I'm raising my children. I'm not raising them to assert myself. I'm raising them to become better, to fulfil destiny, and in that process they're going to make mistakes so it's not about me.

This is how you can pay into that emotional bank:

There are simple things you can do to build your child's emotional bank. Every time you build your emotional life on the weakness of others, you empower those weaknesses, and you disempower yourself. But if you focus on your circle of influence - on doing what you can to build your emotional bank account, to build a relationship of trust and unconditional love, you dramatically increase the ability to influence others positively.

Now, these are some specific ideas on how you can make deposits to your children's account or your spouse's account without having to withdraw

- **Being Kind.**

Kindness goes a long way toward building a relationship of trust and unconditional love. Think about the impact of your own family using words and phrases like 'thank you', 'please excuse me', and 'may I help you?' Sometimes it's just in your unexpected act of kindness: helping your children do the dishes, etc. Some nights it was my daughter and I in the kitchen trying to do the chores. One time we finished and she said "Oh Mommy thank you so much this was just so good." Saying things as simple as I love you in the middle of the day, is an expression of simple gratitude.

Learn to randomly express love and gratitude in simple ways like "Oh thank you so much Ayo for bringing up this water for me oh I just love you." Simple things show your recognition not just at times of special achievement or occasions like birthdays. Do you know that research says that humans require 12 Hugs per day? We all need different forms of emotional nourishment from other people and sometimes spiritual nourishment through meditation or prayers.

Simple words. The way you even communicate with your child. If you pay into that emotional bank, when there's an issue, it will be a walk in the park.

I read a book about a woman who grew up in poverty and contention and then she started working in a prestigious hotel where the entire staff had a culture of courtesy, I call it honour. The woman started to look at the procedure of how people treated them with kindness and one day she decided to try it out and brought it home to her family. She began to do little acts of kindness for her family members. She would use positive language, using gentle words, that are kind, just like she did at work and it was so transformational for both her and her family and they began a new intergenerational cycle.

I remember one of my clients telling me that in their family, what they do is that they take turns every morning to compliment one another and one of those mornings the son was running down the stairs and when they asked him why he was running, he said: "It's my turn to compliment everybody today."

This is one of the most important dimensions of kindness and it expresses such an important deposit to make and to teach in a family so being kind can be in the words that you speak or gestures like hugging.

- **Apologizing**

Perhaps there's nothing that tests our proactive capacity as much as saying 'I am sorry' to the other person. In my home, you don't say "sorry" you say "I am sorry", you cannot just say sorry. You intentionally say sorry and if your security is based on your image or your position or your being right to apologize, you need to step back and ask yourself can I apologize?

My husband is a marriage counsellor and its one of the things that he teaches in communication class, and it's one of the things that we practice. Whenever we disagree with others, we need to quickly agree with them, not on the issue of disagreement because that will be compromising our integrity, but on the right to disagree - to see it the way they see it. Otherwise, to protect themselves, they will put us in a mental emotional prison in their mind. When there is a problem, one of the things that we acknowledge is "I know I want to agree with you", that's one of the biggest things.

Apologizing or saying "I'm sorry" is not just about saying I'm sorry, the first thing you want to do when you disagree with people in your family is to quickly agree with them. Agreeing with them is not the issue of the disagreement, it's not you compromising or about integrity, but the right to disagree.

I was talking with my children and we had a disagreement because my son felt he could swim and did not need an adult to supervise him, when we were done with the back and forth, he was a bit sad and I said to him, "I agree with you on this issue but not on the issue of you going alone to the pool" and then I said, "you also have the right to disagree".

You need to learn to agree immediately with them otherwise to protect themselves, we will put them in a mental emotional prison in their home and they won't be released from that prison until you fully acknowledge your mistake not allowing them the right to disagree. Everybody has a right to disagree and if you want to talk about apologizing to people, you need to do it without labelling, you need to consult your conscience and tap into the moral and ethical sense. You need to have a sense of what is happening, and what would be better and you have to act on it. If you don't focus on this, you will neglect the entire efforts, it will break down and you will end up trying to defend, to justify, to explain, to cover up for offensive behaviour in some way.

Don't make your apology superficial, you need to be sincere about your apologies. There is something called apology language and everybody does not receive an apology the same way.

- **Being loyal to family members who are not present**

One of the toughest, most important deposits you can make in your family or an entire family, is to adopt a fundamental value and commitment, which is to be loyal to family members who are not present. In other words, talk about others as if they were present that doesn't mean you are unaware of their weaknesses. If you talk about those weaknesses, you do it in such a responsible and constructive way that you will not be ashamed to have those you're talking about overhear your conversation.

I remember a client who came asking about their 18-year-old son who had irritating habits, that sometimes the siblings would sit and talk about the guy and one day I said "Can you also stop talking about this guy behind his back?" One of the things he does is that he hurts the whole family, you're the whole family and that's what we don't even understand. The message sent to one is truly sent to all because everyone is one and if you treat one that way, all it takes is to change the circumstances and you will treat them the same way too, that's why it's important to be loyal to those not present. When you criticize your children, you break down the family system and when there is a problem to be solved, there is already a bias.

One of the things that I do with my children is that if there's a problem, we don't call you to criticize the other siblings, we solve problems. If you do that, you are going to be selling the idea that 'if I'm also in this position, the same thing will happen' and it gives you negatives in the emotional bank.
To be loyal, you need to be self-aware, you need to have a sense of consciousness of what is right, and you need to have the fortitude to make what should happen, happen. If you are interested in creating a transformational family, you need to put your foot forward and take some steps that are not as easy as they look. The idea is to make everybody feel comfortable and solve problems together. So, a message sent to one is truly sent to all because everyone is one. It is very important, to be loyal to those not present. It is a very clearly proactive choice.

- **Making and keeping promises**
It's hard to come to a deposit that has more impact on a family than making and keeping promises. Just think about how much excitement, how much anticipation and hope is created by a promise. The promises we make in the family are the most vital and often the most tender promises of all. The most foundational promise

we ever make to another human being is the vow inside marriage. In marriage, that's the biggest and ultimate promise and equal to it is a promise we inexplicitly have with our children, particularly when they are little. Promises to take care of them, to nurture them, that's why divorce and abandonments are such painful withdrawals. Those involved often feel as though the ultimate promises have been broken so when these things occur, it becomes even more important to make deposits that will help rebuild bridges of confidence and trust.

This is also about your relationship with people as a friend. Be careful how you sit amongst the congregation of the scornful like the Bible will say, where people just sit and scorn people, be careful about that. It messes up effective communication because there's always a bias when those things happen.

- **Forgiving**

You need to learn to forgive. It's not the snake bite that does the serious damage, but chasing the snake that drives the poison to the heart. Are you chasing the snake when there's a problem? If you are going to ensure that you are going to solve problems using effective communication in your family, then you must look at these things critically and say to yourself, "I am here because I want to build a proactive family".

There is no way to have a rich rewarding family relationship without understanding. Relationships can be superficial, transactional, and functional. Most transactional, just a few functional. You rarely see transformational relationships. You can't build a transformational relationship without effective communication values.

HOW FAMILIES FUNCTION

Families function differently according to what they want to achieve, their vision, and their goals. This can be categorized into the following:
1. Superficial family relationships
2. Transactional family relationships
3. Functional family relationships
4. Transformational family relationships

1. Superficial Family Relationships

Superficial family relationships, while serving some functions within the family system, come with their own set of disadvantages. These relationships, which often lack depth and authenticity, can hinder the emotional well-being and growth of family members. Here's an exploration of the drawbacks of superficial family relationships and the importance of building genuine connections within families:

Disadvantages of Superficial Family Relationships:

Emotional Distance: Superficial relationships can lead to emotional distance between family members. The lack of authentic communication and deep connections can make it difficult for family members to understand each other's emotions, struggles, and needs.

Missed Opportunities for Support: Superficial relationships may prevent family members from seeking or offering meaningful support during challenging times. When genuine connections are lacking, family members may feel isolated in their problems.

Surface-Level Conflict Resolution: In superficial relationships, conflicts are often addressed on the surface without delving into underlying issues. This can lead to unresolved tensions and ongoing misunderstandings.

Limited Understanding: Superficial relationships may lead to a limited understanding of one another's personalities, desires, and values. This lack of understanding can hinder the development of empathy and shared experiences.

The Importance of Genuine Connections in Families:

- Emotional Fulfillment: Building real relationships within families is essential for emotional fulfilment. Authentic connections allow family members to share their joys, sorrows, and experiences more deeply, creating a more nurturing environment.
- Conflict Resolution and Growth: Genuine connections enable family members to address conflicts in a more meaningful way. Open communication and emotional understanding can lead to the resolution of issues and personal growth.
- Building Trust: Real relationships are built on trust and honesty. Trust is the foundation of a healthy family dynamic, allowing family members to rely on one another and feel secure in their connections.
- Cultural and Family Traditions: Strong, genuine connections within the family contribute to the preservation and continuation of cultural and family traditions. These connections pass on values and practices that are important to the family's identity.
- Adaptation and Resilience: Genuine family relationships help the family adapt to change and build resilience. When family members have authentic connections, they are better equipped to face challenges together and support each other through transitions.

In conclusion, while superficial family relationships may serve ceremonial and social functions, they often fall short of meeting the emotional and personal growth needs of family members. Building genuine connections within the family is essential for creating a nurturing, supportive, and harmonious environment where family members can thrive emotionally and adapt to the changing dynamics of life. Prioritizing open and authentic communication is the first step toward transforming superficial relationships into meaningful and lasting bonds within the family

2. Transactional family relationships

While serving practical functions, can pose significant challenges to the well-being of family members. Here are the disadvantages and reasons for avoiding transactional family relationships:

Disadvantages of Transactional Family Relationships:
- Emotional Disconnect: Transactional family relationships often prioritize exchanges of material or non-material resources over emotional connection. Family members may feel emotionally distant from each other, leading to a lack of intimacy and empathy.
- Conditional Support: Support in transactional relationships may be conditional, based on the expectation of reciprocation. This can lead to feelings of indebtedness and strain in family relationships.
- Lack of Authenticity: Family members may feel compelled to adhere to transactional norms, preventing them from expressing their true emotions or opinions. This lack of authenticity can hinder genuine communication.
- Stress and Pressure: The constant need for transactions and reciprocation can create stress and pressure on family members. The fear of failing to fulfil transactional expectations can be overwhelming.
- Conflict Over Resources: Disputes may arise when family members perceive imbalances or unfairness in resource distribution. These disputes can escalate into conflicts that strain family relationships.

Reasons to Avoid Transactional Family Relationships:
- Emotional Well-being: Genuine family relationships prioritize emotional well-being. Avoiding transactional relationships allows family members to connect on a deeper emotional level, fostering trust, empathy, and understanding.
- Unconditional Support: In non-transactional relationships, support is given without the expectation of reciprocation. This creates an environment of unconditional love and care, where family members can rely on one another in times of need.

- Authentic Communication: Non-transactional relationships encourage authentic and open communication. Family members can express their thoughts, feelings, and concerns freely, strengthening the bonds that tie them together.
- Reduced Stress: By avoiding transactional relationships, family members can reduce the stress and pressure associated with constantly meeting transactional expectations. This promotes mental and emotional well-being.
- Resolution of Conflicts: Non-transactional relationships prioritize resolving conflicts through communication and compromise rather than material exchanges. This leads to healthier conflict resolution and stronger family connections.

3. Functional Family Relationships

These drawbacks can arise when the focus on functionality overshadows emotional needs and individual growth. Here are some disadvantages of functional family relationships:
- Emotional Disconnect: In highly functional families, the focus on tasks and responsibilities may overshadow emotional connections. Family members may feel emotionally distant from one another, leading to a lack of intimacy and understanding.
- Lack of Flexibility: Functional family relationships can sometimes become rigid, with set roles and responsibilities that leave little room for flexibility or personal growth. This rigidity can stifle creativity and adaptability within the family.
- Role Strain: The pressure to fulfil specific roles and responsibilities within a functional family can lead to role strain. Family members may feel overwhelmed or stressed due to the demands of their assigned tasks.
- Emotional Suppression: To maintain functionality, family members may suppress their emotions, leading to a buildup of

unresolved feelings and potential emotional explosions in the future.

- Conflict Avoidance: Functional families may prioritize harmony to such an extent that they avoid conflicts at all costs. While this may seem positive, it can lead to unaddressed issues and a lack of resolution for important family matters.
- Overemphasis on Efficiency: An obsession with efficiency and functionality can sometimes overshadow the importance of nurturing personal growth, creativity, and individual expression within the family.

It's important to strike a balance between functionality and emotional connection within the family. While functional relationships ensure the smooth running of the household, addressing the disadvantages by nurturing emotional connections, promoting flexibility, and acknowledging personal growth is crucial for maintaining a healthy family dynamic.

4. Transformational Family Relationships

Transformational family relationships are often considered the cornerstone of how a family operates and thrives. These relationships inspire personal growth, facilitate change, and contribute significantly to the overall well-being of family members. Here's how transformational family relationships play a crucial role in how a family runs:

- Support for Personal Growth: Transformational family relationships are marked by their unwavering support for each member's personal growth and development. Family members act as each other's champions, encouraging and nurturing individual strengths, talents, and aspirations. This support is the catalyst for self-discovery and the pursuit of dreams and goals. Imagine a teenager who aspires to become an artist. In a transformational family, they are met with enthusiasm and support from their family, who provide the resources and encouragement needed to develop their artistic talents.

- Fostering Self-Expression: In transformational family relationships, open self-expression is not just encouraged; it's celebrated. Family members feel safe to share their aspirations, fears, and dreams without the fear of judgment. This fosters an environment of authenticity and self-acceptance. For instance, an adult family member openly discusses their desire to change careers within the family. Instead of judgment, they receive support, advice, and the space to share their concerns and dreams.
- Empowerment: Transformational relationships empower family members to set and pursue their goals, whatever they may be. Family members feel confident and supported in their endeavours, whether it's a career change, educational pursuit, or personal project. A family member, inspired by their transformational family, decides to pursue a long-held dream of starting a small business. They find not only emotional support but also help in planning and executing their business idea.
- Shared Values and Vision: Transformational family relationships are often grounded in shared values and a common vision for personal and family growth. These shared values create a strong sense of purpose, motivating family members to work together toward their goals. Example: A family's shared value of education leads to a collective vision of each family member completing higher education. This shared vision becomes a driving force for academic achievement within the family.
- Conflict Resolution: In transformational family relationships, conflicts are viewed as opportunities for growth and understanding. Family members approach conflicts intending to resolve them constructively. This approach not only resolves conflicts but also strengthens the bond among family members. Example: A disagreement arises within the family about how to manage finances. In a transformational family, the family members engage in open and honest communication, addressing the issue to find a mutually beneficial solution and ultimately deepening their understanding of one another.

Impact: Transformational family relationships are at the heart of how a family operates, fostering personal growth, emotional well-being, and unity. They inspire and empower family members to fulfil their potential, making the family a nurturing environment for individual success and collective happiness. Ultimately, transformational relationships help the family run smoothly and harmoniously, with each member contributing to the overall well-being of the family unit.

CHAPTER 3

UNLOCKING TRANSFORMATIONAL FAMILY DYNAMICS: Shifting From Transactional To Transformational Relationships

Most of the family relationships we have today are either transactional, superficial, or just "functional" nothing transformational or deeply satisfying. And many times families are transactional more than anything. The "I am here for something you offer" kind of relationship. "If you don't offer anything, I won't offer either."

It's all about "doing" only when someone "does" and when they don't, everyone carries on with their "independence".

Unfortunately, no transformational family thrives on this method. I know it may seem to work for you but parenting is not about "do whatever works for you, don't judge us." It's about what is best for the family. And what is best for any family is interdependence and mutuality. These are the things that keep your family, making it transformational and deeply satisfying. And this will require that everyone give their best at all times.

Families that thrive, not just function, require principles, not a case of whatever works for you. They work on instituted instructions not just opinions and at the core of this is effective communication.

In the vast tapestry of life, few relationships hold the profound significance of those within our families. They are the bedrock of our existence, the source of our earliest memories, and the harbour to which we return in times of joy and sorrow. Yet, amidst the complexity of these bonds, it's not uncommon for family dynamics to become entangled in the mundane routines of daily life.

As we begin this journey of transformation, take a moment to reflect on what your families mean to you. Think about the shared laughter, tears, and the countless stories that make up the fabric of your family history.

Within this intricate web of relationships, there is a world of untapped potential waiting to be explored.

Consider for a moment, the current state of your family dynamics. Are your interactions primarily transactional in nature? Are they characterized by the exchange of chores, responsibilities, and conditional expectations?

Do you find that routine and habit have taken centre stage in your family life?

If you answered yes to any of these questions, you're not alone. Many families find themselves caught in the gravitational pull of transactional interactions. These interactions, while necessary in daily life, can sometimes overshadow the essence of what family truly means. In the hustle and bustle of modern existence, it's easy to slip into a mode where familial interactions become predictable and perhaps even mechanical.

But fear not, this chapter marks the first step in your journey of transformation. It's an opportunity to rekindle the spirit of your family relationships, to reinvigorate your connection with those who matter most to you. Together, we'll explore the transformative potential that lies within your family dynamics.

This journey is not about starting from scratch; it's about building upon the foundation you already have. Your family's uniqueness, its quirks, its shared experiences – all of these contribute to the tapestry of your relationships.

I'm here to help you uncover the hidden gems, to breathe new life into your family connections, and to guide you toward creating lasting memories and legacies.

In this chapter, expect questions and perspectives that will prompt you to think deeply about your family dynamics.

-What does family mean to you?

-What are the patterns that define your interactions?

-How can you transition from the transactional to the transformational?

Throughout this book, you'll see insights, stories, and practical techniques that will guide you toward realizing the transformational potential that lies within your family relationships. We invite you to embrace this journey with an open heart and a willingness to explore the depths of your family dynamics.

Your family's journey will be a unique and deeply personal one, but the principles and strategies explored in this book will serve as your guiding stars. The transformation we aim for is not an overnight change but a gradual shift that can lead to profound improvements in the quality of your family life.

This chapter marks the beginning of a profound transformation, one that will open doors to richer, more meaningful family relationships. The journey is a tribute to the importance of families, as they are not just units bound by blood but the architects of our individual and collective well-being. Together, we take the first step towards unlocking transformational family dynamics, setting the stage for the chapters to come.

UNDERSTANDING THE TRANSACTIONAL TRAP

You can't embark on the journey of transforming family dynamics without first understanding the trap of transactional relationships, because it serves as a crucial stepping stone. It invites us to delve into the intricate workings of the "transactional trap," a common pattern that many families unintentionally find themselves ensnared in.

Consider the story of the Okonkwo family, who recently joined the "Intentional Parent Academy" in their quest to become more intentional parents. The Okonkwos, like many families, found themselves entrapped in a set of routines and patterns that defined their daily lives. This is a story that may resonate with you as well.

Transactional Relationships Within the Okonkwo Family

For the Okonkwos, family life had become largely transactional. Mornings were a whirlwind of getting the children ready for school, juggling work schedules, and ensuring all the household chores were checked off. The kids received allowances for their chores, and in turn, they adhered to a structured routine. And the parents would always refer to how they need to get it right so they can take care of them in old age.

-Conditional Love and Affection
In their pursuit of efficiency, the Okonkwos had inadvertently attached conditions to their love and affection. Children were praised and rewarded for completing chores and meeting academic goals. The unspoken rule seemed to be, "We love you, but you must earn it."

-Lack of Open Communication
Another significant feature of the Okonkwos family's transactional dynamic was the lack of open communication. Conversations were often centred around task-related topics. Discussions about emotions, dreams, and aspirations were rare.

The Pitfalls of the Transactional Trap
What the Okonkwos, and countless other families who fall into this trap, may not have fully realized is that transactional relationships, while efficient for managing daily life, often come with inherent pitfalls:

-Emotional Disconnect
By emphasizing routines and rewards, transactional relationships can create an emotional disconnect. Family members may begin to feel that they are fulfilling roles rather than nurturing genuine connections.

-Stagnation and Limited Growth

In the Okonkwos family, the strict chore-based system inadvertently limited the children's opportunities for personal growth and exploration. It hindered their ability to develop individual interests and passions.

-Conflict and Tension
Conditional love and rigid routines can lead to conflicts and tension. In the Okonkwos family, this was most apparent when the children felt they were not meeting their parents' expectations, which resulted in arguments and disagreements.

CASE STUDY: The Okonkwos' Transformation

The Okonkwos' story is not one of despair but of hope. They realized that while their transactional system was efficient in some ways, it was not nurturing the strong family connections they desired. Through their involvement with the "Intentional Parent Academy," they began to explore the benefits of transitioning toward transformational family dynamics.

This case study illustrates that, like the Okonkwos, families can recognize the transactional trap and take active steps to transform their relationships into something richer, more fulfilling, and deeply connected.

WHAT ARE TRANSFORMATIONAL FAMILY DYNAMICS?

Transformational family dynamics are a paradigm shift from transactional routines to a deeper, more profound way of relating within families. They emphasize emotional connection, personal growth, and mutual support. Imagine a family where love and acceptance are freely given, where each member is encouraged to thrive and where resilience is cultivated through shared experiences. Transformational families prioritize these elements above all.

Benefits of Transformational Relationships within Families

There are significant benefits of transformational relationships within families, which are well-illustrated by the Abiodun family, who have actively embraced transformation.

1. Enhanced Emotional Well-being

The Abioduns, a family of five, describe the shift from transactional to transformational dynamics as life-altering. By placing emotional connection at the core of their family interactions, they noticed a significant improvement in emotional well-being. There was less stress, more laughter, and a deep sense of contentment that transcended the ordinary. They used simple tools of connection to achieve this. At the Intentional Parent Inner Circle program, we are very big on connections not just routines.

2. Individual Growth

In the Smith family, transformational dynamics fostered an environment where each family member was encouraged to pursue their passions and goals. The children were actively engaged in extracurricular activities they were passionate about, and the parents supported their endeavours. This nurtured personal growth and self-actualization among family members.

3. Resilience

The Yinusas described how the strength of their transformational family dynamics became evident during times of challenges. When one family member faced a health crisis, the entire family rallied together. Their shared emotional bonds and unwavering support were instrumental in navigating through adversity, ultimately leading to a full recovery.

REAL-LIFE SUCCESS STORIES

Beyond the Smiths, there are countless success stories of families who have transitioned from transactional to transformational dynamics. Consider the Garbos family, who decided to set aside a weekly "family night" dedicated to bonding and quality time. These nights featured activities that allowed open communication, the expression of emotions, and the exploration of common interests. The Garbos found that these nights strengthened their family bonds and created lasting memories.

Another powerful example is the Garcia family. Recognizing the impact of transformational dynamics, they launched a tradition of sharing stories from their cultural heritage. These stories were not mere anecdotes but heartfelt narratives that strengthened the family's connection to their roots, culture, and history.
Such stories inspire and show that transformational family dynamics are within reach, no matter the family's background or composition.

TRANSFORMATIONAL RELATIONSHIPS
VS.
TRANSACTIONAL RELATIONSHIPS

The differences between transformational and transactional relationships are stark. Transactional relationships may prioritize routine tasks, whereas transformational relationships focus on emotional well-being, individual growth, and mutual support. They elevate the essence of what it means to be part of a family.
There are a couple of strategies and tools that can help you cultivate these transformational dynamics within your own family. Through these insights and practical exercises, you'll be empowered

to enrich your family relationships, replacing transactional habits with transformational connections. The journey is just beginning, and the potential for a more fulfilling family life is within your grasp.

PRACTICAL TOOLS FOR TRANSFORMATION

The journey to transform your family dynamics from transactional to transformational is a path filled with opportunities for growth and connection. The following tools are fail proof ways to make this shift within your family.

Effective Communication: Listening and Expressing

-Tool 1: Active Listening

Effective communication is at the heart of transformational relationships. Active listening is a technique that fosters deeper understanding and connection within families. It requires giving your full attention when someone is speaking, without judgment or interruption. The listener seeks to understand the speaker's perspective and feelings. Practice this technique during family discussions to encourage empathy and create a safe space for open communication.

Example: During family dinner, designate a "listening circle" where each family member has a turn to share their day's experiences without interruption. The rest of the family practices active listening, maintaining eye contact, nodding to show understanding, and refraining from offering advice or judgment until the speaker has finished sharing.

-Tool 2: Expressing Emotions

Transformational family dynamics thrive on the open expression of emotions. Encourage family members to express their feelings and thoughts honestly. Share your own emotions and thoughts with your family. By creating an environment where emotions are acknowledged and respected, you'll build trust and promote emotional intimacy.

Example: Implement a weekly "emotional check-in" during a family meeting. Each family member takes a turn expressing their emotions, whether positive or negative. Encourage open and honest sharing without fear of judgment or criticism. This exercise helps family members become more comfortable with expressing their feelings and it promotes emotional intimacy.

Building Trust and Empathy
-Tool 3: Trust-Building Activities

Trust is the cornerstone of transformational relationships. Engage in trust-building activities with your family. These can include trust falls, collaborative projects, or sharing vulnerabilities. By working together to build trust, you'll strengthen your emotional bonds.

Example: Engage in team-building activities that require trust. A classic example is the "trust fall," where one family member stands with their back to the rest of the family, crosses their arms over their chest, and falls backwards, trusting that the others will catch them. Such activities build physical and emotional trust.

-Tool 4: Empathy Development

Empathy is the ability to understand and share the feelings of another. Teach your family members to practice empathy by putting themselves in each other's shoes. Encourage discussions about emotions, and ask family members to consider how others might be feeling in different situations.

Example: Create a family game night where you play games that require perspective-taking and empathy. For instance, play "The Perspective Game," where each family member takes a turn sharing a challenging experience they've had, and the others must listen and offer empathetic responses.

Setting and Pursuing Shared Family Goals

-Tool 5: Family Goal Setting

Transformational families often have shared goals that guide their interactions. Sit down as a family and discuss what you want to achieve together. These goals can be related to personal development, shared experiences, or contributions to your community. Setting and pursuing these goals as a family can provide a sense of purpose and unity.

Example: Have a family sit-down to discuss goals. During this discussion you may for instance plan a family vacation to a destination that excites everyone. Ensure you establish clear objectives, responsibilities and timelines to achieve this goal. Revisit your progress regularly and celebrate the milestones as you go along.

-Tool 6: Collaborative Achievement

Celebrate your family's achievements together. Recognize the value of teamwork and cooperation in reaching your goals. Acknowledge each family member's contributions and share the sense of accomplishment that comes from working together.

Example: Suppose one of your family goals is to create a vegetable garden. Assign specific tasks to family members based on their interests and abilities. As each task is completed, acknowledge and celebrate the progress together. When the garden yields its first harvest, have a family dinner featuring dishes made from your produce.

Nurturing Individual Growth within the Family Unit

-Tool 7: Supporting Individual Passions

Each family member is unique in their interests and passions. Encourage and support individual pursuits within the family unit. This can involve providing time, and resources, or simply being an enthusiastic cheerleader for each other's endeavours.

Example: If one family member is passionate about art, create a dedicated space for their art supplies and creations. Encourage art-related activities and, if possible, attend their art exhibitions or showcase their work within the family. This support demonstrates that individual passions are valued within the family.

-Tool 8: Encouraging Lifelong Learning

Cultivate a love for learning within your family. Discuss books, new skills, and interests. Encourage family members to pursue education and personal growth, whether through formal education or self-directed learning. Make learning an integral part of your family culture.

Example: Designate a "Learning Day" where each family member gets to choose an educational activity for the family. It could be visiting a museum, watching a documentary, or even cooking a traditional dish from another culture. Emphasize the joy of learning and exploration as a family value.

These practical tools and exercises are designed to be accessible and effective, promoting transformational relationships within your family. By incorporating these practices into your daily life, you can gradually transition from transactional interactions to transformational relationships, creating deeper connections, improved communication, and greater personal and collective growth among family members. The journey is unfolding, and these tools will serve as your compass for transformation.

CREATING AND SUSTAINING YOUR FAMILY LEGACY

As we progress on the path of transforming your family dynamics, it's essential to remember that the ultimate goal is not just to enrich your current family interactions but to leave a lasting impact for generations to come. This is where the concept of "family legacy" becomes paramount.

A family legacy is not merely about material wealth or possessions. It encompasses the values, stories, traditions, and emotional connections that you pass down to your children, grandchildren, and beyond. It is a testament to your family's identity and the mark you leave on the world.

Why Family Legacy Matters
Creating and sustaining a family legacy is the pinnacle of transformational family dynamics. It's the realisation that your family is not just for fun but for fulfilment and that it's not just a collection of individuals. It's an entity with its history, beliefs, and contributions to society. Your legacy reflects the values and principles you hold dear and provides a blueprint for future generations.

Preserving Family Stories and Traditions
Think about the stories you heard from your grandparents or the traditions your family has cherished for generations. These are the threads that weave your family history together. By preserving these narratives and traditions, you not only honour your past but also provide a sense of identity and belonging to your children and grandchildren.

Financial Planning and Wealth Management
While financial wealth is just one facet of a family legacy, it plays a critical role in ensuring the continuity of your family's values and goals. Establishing a comprehensive financial plan, including wills, trusts, and estate planning, can help safeguard your assets and facilitate a smooth transition of wealth to future generations. However, remember that financial wealth is only meaningful when it aligns with your family's values and mission.

Philanthropy and Giving Back
A central aspect of creating a family legacy is the notion of giving back. By engaging in philanthropic activities and community involvement, you instill a sense of social responsibility in your family. This not only benefits the community but also serves as a powerful

lesson in empathy and compassion for your children and grandchildren.

Education and Skill Development

Your family legacy is built on a foundation of knowledge and growth. Invest in the education and skill development of your family members. Encourage them to pursue their passions and interests, and mentor them as they explore new horizons. Education is not just about academics; it's about instilling a love for lifelong learning and personal development.

Family Governance Structure

Creating a family governance structure helps establish a framework for decision-making, roles, and responsibilities within the family. It ensures transparency and shared values. I shared on how to create this in my book "Discipline is Not an Emergency". Holding regular family meetings allows for open discussions about important matters and reinforces the family legacy's guiding principles.

Family Traditions and Rituals

Family traditions and rituals are the heartbeat of your legacy. These are the celebrations, ceremonies, and customs that bind generations together. Whether it's a holiday tradition, a yearly family reunion, or a special way of marking milestones, these rituals create a sense of continuity and unity within the family.

Communication and Conflict Resolution

A crucial aspect of a thriving family legacy is effective communication and conflict resolution. Your legacy should include a culture of open dialogue, active listening, and constructive conflict resolution. This ensures that your family continues to evolve and grow, adapting to changing times and challenges.

Document and Record-Keeping

Preserving your family legacy requires diligent documentation. Keep comprehensive records of family history, values, and financial matters. Utilize technology to safeguard important documents and memories, ensuring they remain accessible to future generations.

Mentorship and Leadership Transition

Mentorship is the key to nurturing leadership within your family. Encourage younger family members to learn from their elders and take on leadership roles. Plan for the transition of leadership within family businesses or other family initiatives. This ensures that your legacy lives on through capable hands.

Adaptability and Flexibility

Finally, remember that adaptability and flexibility are integral to sustaining a family legacy. As your family grows and evolves, be open to change and innovation. Encourage new generations to contribute their ideas and perspectives, keeping your legacy relevant and vibrant.

Creating and sustaining your family legacy is the ultimate goal of transformational family dynamics. It's about building a narrative that transcends generations, leaving a profound mark on the world and instilling the values and principles you hold dear. The legacy you create will serve as a testament to the strength and unity of your family, ensuring that your influence continues to shape the lives of your descendants for years to come.

CHAPTER 4

SOLVING FAMILY PROBLEMS THROUGH EFFECTIVE COMMUNICATION USING DIFFERENT TOOLS

"A fool takes no pleasure in understanding but only in expressing his opinion". - Prov 18: 2

Many times we play the fool when it comes to our families. All we talk about and think about is expressing our opinions, we don't want to understand. The Bible calls that being a fool, if you take no pleasure in understanding and learning in wisdom and it's just about expressing your own opinion.

At the heart of every family's pain is misunderstanding. As someone who has advocated for families and run group family counselling for years now, I've seen this first-hand. And this is what this verse of the bible is talking about. Do not forget if you are interested in building a transformational family then you will do things differently, you would apply effective communication principles because that is the heart of every conversation of every family that is built differently.

"How well we communicate is not determined by how well we say things but how well we understand it and how well we know we are understood".   Andrew Grove Engineer CEO.

One thing I have realized when it comes to communication is that it's not just about what you say or how you say it, it is how well the people you are saying it to, understand it. Many times in many families, we complain that our children are not listening, have you asked yourself am "I communicating effectively?"

Communication is a two-way process. For communication to happen, it must be conveyed to the sender. I met a woman who had applied what she learnt on how to treat people from her workplace, a luxury hotel, in her home and she saw how that transformed the system in her home. It's interesting how we all practice effective communication outside, we talk to people nicely, we treat them well, and we honour people then when we come home we talk to our spouses and children differently. That's why when people ask me to define honour I say that, "honour is customer service brought home".

Communication is conveying a message to another person to be understood. The word communication comes from the word communique in Latin which means to share, to exchange, to consult one another, to confer, to participate. It means to get in contact with a person. When you are talking to your children ask yourself, "Is what I'm doing communication and exchange?"

Many times we don't communicate, we just instruct. We do forget that our communication should be a two-way thing, most times we are talking over the heads of people, and there's no participation so you just talk. In most of our families, remember we're talking about effective communication in families, there's no participation, there's no consultation, there is no exchange. It's just criticism, judgment, and instructions, and that's not effective communication.

Effective communication is a product or process. It is a skill. It is a product of the climate. It's a product of the connection, relationship, and hard work you put in. There is no effective communication without you thinking of how, what it is that you put in, is impacting others. Some people say children just learn to talk. The question is what exactly are they talking about? What are they saying? Talking doesn't necessarily mean you're communicating. You can talk and talk and not be able to communicate.

Many times, in our homes we are talking but we're not communicating and that's why when it comes to effective communication, we struggle because you would say "I have been talking."
I hear parents say to me "I've been talking to my children and they don't listen."   Yes, you
may have been talking, but no, you have not been communicating

effectively. Hearing you is one thing, actually understanding you is another thing entirely. You talk to your teenager like you're talking to your 20-year-old, you talk to your 20-year-old like you're talking to a 30-year-old and of course, there is always a hint because of course that doesn't always work.

Communication is not what we say, it is what the other person understands. Any communication that you offer that is not understood, believe me, you didn't communicate and that is why many of the times when you communicate aggressively, everybody misunderstands and the communication line breaks down completely. So you can't communicate so that's why many times when you raise your voice, people you are talking to try to defend themselves. I remember an incident that happened with my very close friend I was trying to tell her that what she did was wrong, she was of course trying to defend herself and it was wrong understood but you know when we were talking she said why didn't you think of the way it was said and that's a very valid point so it was okay for me at that time to think that I needed to talk about my own.

Remember what the quote from the Bible said, the fool takes no pleasure in understanding but only in expressing his opinion. Many times we are like that, we just want to express our opinion, and we don't want to be understood, that comes from Proverbs 18:2, A fool takes no pleasure in understanding but only in expressing his opinion and at that time while I was talking, I just wanted to express my opinion, many of us find ourselves in those places with your opinion, you don't even want to understand and many of the times there's something to understand. This is a very instructive food for thought.

HINDRANCES TO EFFECTIVE COMMUNICATION IN FAMILIES

The single biggest problem in communication is the illusion that it has taken place ~George Bernard Shaw -Nobel prize-winning playwright.

I wanted to think about it slowly, the single biggest problem in communication is the illusion that it has even taken place at all because a lot of the time we communicate but many of the time it doesn't even take place and that's what happens in our families. The first day I came in contact with this quote, it struck me and that is the biggest problem we think we've communicated but we haven't.

Communication is a complex process.
What is the impact?
What is it about?
Who says what to whom?

Speaking well or forming arguments is not sufficient to be a good communicator.

To explain the complexity of communication, I often use the example of the phone game when I do live training. I remember in those days it was hospital setting trainings and I realized that many of the times even medical practitioners communicate with their patients and they don't understand what they say so when we do the phone conversation game. The phone game is an Arabian game called the fungi.

How does it work? I use it to illustrate how communication can get distorted from one person to another if you are in a place where there are 10 people for instance and you want to see the process of the distortedness of communication, tell one person I want you to go outside and buy bread and by the time this gets to the last 10th person you'll be hearing things like you said you will give me money let me go and buy bread, any time you do it, you will see how even from the second person these conversations begins to deteriorate.

It is important to understand who says what to whom and what is the impact. I'm talking about this process because we're talking about the family and many of the times we have a breakdown in communication because the family do not take into consideration the breakdown, the complexity of communicating in itself now when it comes to communication processes.

Interferences hinder the communication process and it's a source of distortions.

MISUNDERSTANDINGS, AND MISINTERPRETATIONS:

these are the barriers to effective communication. Several kinds of interference can occur at the various stages of the communication process, and different kinds of issues can occur. It can be different in the frame of reference, the language, the age, do you know that when you're communicating with your children, there can be a misinterpretation because of the age difference, even culture? We live in a different culture and when I teach becoming culturally intelligent for families, I talk about the different cultures from us and our children. Where we grew up and the culture where our children are currently growing up, is different. Your world is different from what it is now, and if you don't understand this you will miss the ability to communicate with them.

EXPERIENCE:

It's important to consider and gauge a person's level of experience when communicating. When you're communicating with your grandmother who is not educated for instance, do you know that the experience can be a hindrance to effective communication?
I got married traditionally some 15 years ago. Before the traditional wedding proper which was the first time The Governor - Kunle Ologe, and his people came to our hometown Awooma-Nma. I had told him that the distance between Owerri town and my village was about 2 hours. This is funny now when I remember it because that

distance is only a 15-minute drive! Gov is a Geographer by training like his Dad Prof. Ologe. The first thing he did was to check the map when I said it, and he gently said "Baby this place can't be more than 15 minutes drive, except the route I am seeing isn't open. My hometown is very central and located on the Owerri - Onitsha expressway, so you can't miss it. I argued and continued to argue. You don't even want to imagine how I argued.

Let me tell you why I never knew that distance was that short. We travelled to my hometown as children and every time we got on the road I slept off. Trust me it felt like 4 hours by the time we arrived. By the time I became a teenager, we didn't travel home a lot anymore. Well, I had to go again at the traditional wedding period. My father is what you call the typical traditional Igbo man, with a big country home in the village, so every traditional rite/ceremony is done at the village home. I think his depth of our cultural heritage helped us understand so much about our home town Awooma-Nma. And also built confidence in us to achieve so much.

On my way to the village this time, I realized that my brother only drove for about 15 minutes and we were at my hometown. In my mind, "How do I tell this man that this trip isn't as far as I earlier said?" This would be my first truth-telling in our marriage. Well, I summoned courage, called Gov and shared my truth moment. Oh, how he laughed at me! This taught me that the fact that you have experienced something doesn't even necessarily mean you have the answer correctly.

I see older people who look at young people teaching and birthing solutions to problems and they continue to argue that they don't know better. Truth is, you might be ignorant like me. Sometimes experience can rob you of learning if you aren't careful. Don't get me wrong, you can learn from experience but it's not necessarily your own experience.

Read that again.

I am also sharing this story to let you understand that your children often can't see the big picture as much as you can see it. Many times, you are saying something and you expect them to see it from the adult perspective but it never sticks. Cut your children some slack, they might be like me thinking that a 15-minute drive is 3 hours. It doesn't make them dumb, they are just being children. Also what you see as a child isn't necessarily enough to draw life perspectives, you need to learn if not you might be arguing ignorantly.

How Experience Hinders Communication

Experience can play a complex role in communication. While experience is generally considered valuable for effective communication, it can also hinder communication in various ways. Here are some ways in which experience can impede communication:

- Assumptions and Preconceptions: When individuals have extensive experience in a particular field or topic, they may make assumptions about what others know or should know. This can lead to communication breakdowns when they use jargon, acronyms, or technical terms, without considering the knowledge level of their audience. The assumption that everyone understands can hinder effective communication, as the audience may feel lost or overwhelmed.
- Overconfidence: Experienced communicators may become overconfident in their abilities, leading to a lack of receptivity to feedback or alternative viewpoints. This overconfidence can stifle open and productive dialogue, as they may be less inclined to listen to others' ideas or consider alternative solutions.
- Loss of Empathy: With experience often comes a sense of expertise, which can lead to a lack of empathy for those who do not share the same level of experience. This can result in a failure to understand or consider the perspectives and concerns of others. As a result, communication may become one-sided and less effective.

- Complexity: In certain fields or industries, experience can lead to an increased understanding of intricate details and nuances. While this depth of knowledge is valuable, it can hinder communication when individuals struggle to simplify and convey complex information in a way that others can understand. The message may become overly technical, making it challenging for those without the same level of expertise to follow.
- Resistance to Change: Experienced individuals may be more resistant to change, particularly if they have found success with their current methods or approaches. This resistance can hinder communication when new ideas or perspectives are met with scepticism or dismissal.
- Ingrained Habits: Over time, people develop habits in their communication styles. These habits can be challenging to change, even if they no longer serve the individual or the organization. Experience can lead to the perpetuation of communication habits that may be outdated or ineffective.
- Biases: Experience can lead to the development of biases or prejudices, particularly in situations where individuals have had negative experiences with certain groups or ideas. These biases can colour communication and impede openness and inclusivity.
- Difficulty in Explaining the Basics: Experienced communicators may struggle to explain basic concepts or ideas to those who are less familiar with the subject matter. They may take foundational knowledge for granted and unintentionally skip over essential information.
- Lack of Adaptability: As individuals accumulate experience, they may become less adaptable in their communication style. This can hinder effective communication in situations that require flexibility and adjustment to the needs of the audience.

To mitigate the hindrances caused by experience in communication, individuals need to remain self-aware, open to feedback, and willing to adapt their communication style to suit the needs of their audience. Balancing the benefits of experience with effective communication skills is key to fostering understanding and collaboration in various contexts.

PHYSICAL INTERFERENCES

How Physical Interferences Impact Effective Communication.
Effective communication is not only about the words spoken but also about the transmission and reception of those words. Physical interferences can disrupt the communication process by interfering with the clear exchange of information and can lead to misunderstandings or communication breakdowns. Here are some ways physical interferences can hinder effective communication:

- Noise Pollution: Environmental noise, such as traffic, construction, loud machinery, or background conversations, can make it challenging to hear and concentrate on a conversation. This can lead to misinterpretations, missed information, or the need to repeat messages. Yelling is also part of noise pollution. Yelling trains your child not to listen to you until you raise your voice and it teaches them to yell back. and any noise in communication makes it ineffective.
- Distance and Space: Physical distance between communicators can hinder communication, particularly in large rooms or over long distances. When individuals are too far apart, it can be challenging to make eye contact, read body language, or hear each other.
- Technology Failures: Technical issues with communication devices, such as phones, computers, or audiovisual equipment, can disrupt communication. This may include dropped calls, poor video quality, or malfunctions during important meetings or discussions.
- Language Barriers: Language barriers, whether due to dialects, accents, or the use of different languages, can impede effective communication. Misunderstandings may arise when individuals have difficulty comprehending one another's speech.

- Visual Obstructions: Physical objects or obstructions in the environment can block visual cues during communication. For example, a pillar in a conference room may obstruct a presenter's view of the audience, making it difficult to gauge their reactions and adjust the message accordingly.
- Inadequate Lighting: Poor lighting conditions can hinder non-verbal communication by obscuring facial expressions and body language. This lack of visibility can lead to misunderstandings or the misinterpretation of emotional cues.
- Physical Disabilities: Individuals with physical disabilities may face communication challenges due to mobility issues or the need for adaptive devices. These obstacles can hinder their ability to engage in face-to-face communication effectively.
- Weather Conditions: Outdoor communication can be greatly affected by weather conditions such as wind, rain, or extreme temperatures. Adverse weather can make it difficult to hear, maintain focus, or conduct conversations comfortably.
- Crowded Environments: Overcrowded spaces can lead to physical congestion, making it difficult to move and communicate freely. This can create stress and frustration, which can hinder effective communication.
- Health and Well-being: Individual health issues, such as hearing impairments or physical discomfort, can impact one's ability to participate fully in a conversation. These health-related challenges can lead to misunderstandings and miscommunications.
- Poor Acoustics: The acoustics of a room or space can impact communication. Echoes, reverberation, or a lack of sound insulation can make it difficult to hear and understand speech.

To overcome physical interferences in communication, it's important to take steps to mitigate these challenges. This may involve finding quieter spaces, ensuring that communication devices are in good working order, using appropriate lighting, and considering the specific needs of individuals with disabilities. Clear and effective communication depends not only on the message and its delivery but also on creating an environment that supports the successful transmission and reception of information.

There can also be YOU as the interference, distraction, and interruption. Many times, your children are talking, and you are on your phone chatting away, there can never be effective communication in that case, it's not possible because there are interferences.

- The Receiver's Internal State

I'm talking to you and you're emotionally down, your attitude, and everything are affected. This can produce snags or even what we call intellectual paralysis that's linked to stress as well.

The receiver's internal state, which includes their emotions, mindset, and physical well-being, can significantly affect communication with a child. Children are often more sensitive to and influenced by the emotional and mental state of the adults or caregivers communicating with them. Here's how the receiver's internal state can impact communication with a child:

- Emotional Tone: Children are highly perceptive of the emotions of adults. If a caregiver is upset, anxious, or frustrated, the child may pick up on these emotions, even if they are not explicitly expressed. This emotional tone can affect how the child interprets and responds to the communication. For example, a child may become anxious or defensive if they sense their caregiver's frustration.
- Empathy and Understanding: The caregiver's ability to empathize with the child's emotions and experiences is crucial for effective communication. If the caregiver is in a positive and empathetic emotional state, they are more likely to understand and validate the child's feelings and needs.
- Patience and Tolerance: A caregiver's level of patience and tolerance can influence their responses to a child's questions, behaviours, and needs. An impatient or easily frustrated adult

may not communicate as effectively with a child, potentially leading to conflicts or misunderstandings.

- Active Listening: The receiver's internal state affects their ability to engage in active listening. If the adult is preoccupied, stressed, or distracted, they may not give the child their full attention, which can hinder effective communication. This also goes to a child, as I shared in my book THE DISCIPLINE THAT WORKS, a misbehaving child is not a listening child.
- Modelling Behavior: Children often learn by observing the behaviours and responses of adults. If a caregiver models positive communication and problem-solving skills through their internal state, the child is more likely to learn and emulate these skills.
- Conflict Resolution: When conflicts arise, the caregiver's internal state plays a critical role in resolving the issue. A calm and composed adult is more likely to handle conflicts with a child constructively, whereas an agitated or stressed adult may struggle to find a resolution.

PHYSICAL WELL-BEING

The caregiver's physical well-being, including factors like fatigue or illness, can influence their energy levels and ability to engage with a child. A tired or unwell adult may not have the same capacity for active and patient communication.

CULTURAL AND PERSONAL BELIEFS

Personal beliefs, cultural backgrounds, and values can also shape the caregiver's internal state, affecting how they communicate with a child. These factors may influence the messages conveyed and the communication style used.

The receiver's internal state has a significant impact on communication with a child. Caregivers and adults involved in a child's life should be mindful of their emotions, attitudes, and overall well-being when interacting with children. Positive, empathetic, patient, and active listening behaviors, foster effective communication and contribute to healthy relationships with children. By maintaining a constructive internal state, adults can create an environment that supports the child's emotional and cognitive development.

THE PRESENCE OF OBSERVERS

The presence of observers can disrupt communication in various ways, depending on the context and the nature of the communication. For instance, when disciplining a child, I say that discipline is a private matter not a public matter because the interferences that happen when it comes to discipline with others being there never gives you the desired result. When you discipline your child and your elder sister for instance or your mother is there, you see that they will call up things not relevant or even deviate from the subject at hand. In the midst of all of this, that communication will never be effective.

Here are some ways in which the presence of observers can interfere with effective communication:

- Self-Consciousness: When individuals are aware that they are being observed, they may become self-conscious. This self-awareness can lead to anxiety, nervousness, and a heightened sense of being "on display." In such a state, people may struggle to express themselves naturally and confidently.

- Inhibition: The knowledge that one's words or actions are being watched can lead to self-censorship. People might withhold information, express themselves less candidly, or refrain from sharing sensitive or controversial topics. This inhibition can hinder open and honest communication.

- Social Pressure: The presence of observers can create social pressure to conform to societal norms or expectations. This pressure can suppress individuality and lead to conformity in communication, making it less authentic and less likely to reflect the true thoughts and feelings of the communicators.

- Distraction: Observers can be distracting, particularly if they are visibly engaged or reacting to the communication. This distraction can disrupt the speaker's train of thought, leading to less focused and coherent communication.

- Loss of Privacy: In personal or sensitive conversations, the presence of observers can make individuals feel that their privacy is compromised. This can result in a reluctance to discuss certain topics or a desire to limit the depth of the conversation.

- Fear of Judgment: Observers, whether intentionally or unintentionally, can convey judgment or evaluation through their body language or facial expressions. This fear of judgment can make individuals cautious and guarded in their communication.

- Communication Barriers: In group settings, observers can physically create barriers between communicators, making it challenging for them to see each other, hear each other clearly, or establish eye contact. These barriers can disrupt the flow of the conversation.

- Reduced Comfort and Trust: The presence of observers can erode the sense of privacy and confidentiality that is often crucial for open and trusting communication. When individuals do not feel secure in the conversation, it can hinder their willingness to share.

- Performance Anxiety: In formal or public speaking situations, such as presentations or speeches, the presence of a larger audience can trigger performance anxiety. This anxiety can affect the speaker's confidence, delivery, and overall effectiveness.
- Misinterpretation: Observers may misinterpret the communication, particularly if they are not fully aware of the context or background information. This misinterpretation can lead to confusion or miscommunication.

Disciplining a child especially in private, without observers, is often recommended for several important reasons:

- Maintaining the Child's Dignity and Self-Esteem: Discipline, when administered in front of others, can be embarrassing and humiliating for a child. It can harm their self-esteem and create a sense of shame. Private discipline allows the child to maintain their dignity.
- Preserving the Parent-Child Relationship: Discipline can be emotionally charged, and addressing it privately allows the parent to focus on the issue at hand without distractions or external pressures. This can help preserve the positive aspects of the parent-child relationship.
- Effective Communication: Private discipline provides a better environment for effective communication. It allows for a calm and focused conversation between the parent and child, where the child can better understand the reasons behind their discipline and the parent's expectations.
- Confidentiality: Some disciplinary situations may involve sensitive or personal issues that should remain confidential. Private discipline ensures that such matters are not discussed or disclosed inappropriately.
- Respect for the Child's Privacy: Just as adults appreciate privacy, children also deserve a certain level of privacy and discretion when it comes to their behaviour and discipline.

Private discipline respects their privacy and allows them to learn without judgment from others.

- Reducing the Risk of Humiliation: Public discipline can lead to humiliation for the child, which can be emotionally damaging. When handled in private, it reduces the risk of the child feeling humiliated in front of peers or family members.

- Child's Safety: In some disciplinary situations, emotions can escalate, leading to potential safety concerns. Handling discipline privately minimizes the chances of a public altercation that may compromise the child's safety.

- Modelling Positive Behavior: When discipline is carried out privately, it serves as a model for positive conflict resolution and problem-solving for the child. They learn that conflicts can be addressed calmly and respectfully.

- Allowing Time for Reflection: Private discipline provides both the parent and child with the opportunity to reflect on the situation. It allows for a cooling-off period, which can be essential for making rational and effective decisions about discipline.

- Consistency and Fairness: Private discipline ensures that the process is consistent and fair. In public situations, parents may feel pressured to act quickly or harshly, which can result in unfair or inconsistent discipline.

- While private discipline is often recommended, it's also crucial to remember that effective discipline should be rooted in love, understanding, and clear communication. I shared a lot on this in the book DISCIPLINE IS NOT AN EMERGENCY. The goal of discipline should be to teach the child right from wrong, promote their personal development, and maintain a healthy parent-child relationship. Discipline should never involve physical harm or emotional abuse, and the child's safety and well-being should always be the top priorities.

MENTAL DISTRACTION

Preoccupying your mind with other topics or preparing an answer instead of listening can largely affect communication. I tell parents to keep what it is that you know first. Once I see a topic that says you can raise your child without hitting them, the first thing is "I already know what the Bible said", you prepared an answer and you haven't listened. That is an obstruction to effective communication and once you do that, you cannot even understand what the other person is saying. Communication interference is a key aspect of communication that you must deal with, both on the person who is receiving it and on the person who is also listening to it.

I need you to understand that when it comes to communication, everything has a whole lot to do with you the person who is communicating. It starts with you that is communicating.

CHAPTER 5

EFFECTIVE COMMUNICATION TOOLS IN FAMILY PROBLEM-SOLVING

How to communicate effectively within the family
Effective communication within the family can be summarized using the "5 Cs" approach:

- **CONNECTION**:
Every great communication begins with connection.
 -Oprah Winfrey

There is no communication without a connection. Many times we want to communicate and one of the problems why we cannot solve a problem is because we do not have a good connection. There are relationships you have in your home, things that are supposed to break you people will happen and you find out that it's just a walkover because of connection.

There is no communication without a connection.

Nurture emotional connections within the family. Promote a sense of togetherness, love, and support. Celebrate each other's achievements, and spend quality time together to strengthen the bonds that tie the family members.

- **CLEAR COMMUNICATION:** Strive for clarity in your communication. Express your thoughts, feelings, and expectations straightforwardly and understandably. Avoid ambiguity and vague language to ensure that your message is easily comprehensible to all family members.

- **CONSIDERATION:** Practice consideration by actively listening to your family members. Pay attention to their concerns and perspectives. Show empathy and respect for their feelings, even if you don't agree with them. Consider their needs and viewpoints in the decision-making process.

- **CONFLICT RESOLUTION:** When conflicts arise, focus on resolving them rather than escalating tensions. Approach conflicts with a willingness to find mutually acceptable solutions. Listen to each other's concerns and engage in constructive discussions to reach resolutions.

- **CONSISTENCY:** Maintain consistency in your communication and behaviour. Consistency fosters predictability and trust within the family. When family members know what to expect, it can lead to a more stable and harmonious environment.

By following the 5 Cs - Clear Communication, Consideration, Conflict Resolution, Consistency, and Connection - you can enhance the quality of communication within your family, leading to healthier and more harmonious relationships.

TOOLS

Effective communication tools in the family are crucial for fostering understanding, resolving conflicts, and maintaining healthy relationships. Here are some communication tools with examples of how they can be applied in typical family interactions:

TOOL 1: ACTIVE LISTENING

Active listening is a communication tool that holds tremendous power in various aspects of life, including within the family. It goes beyond simply hearing words and involves fully engaging with the speaker, both verbally and non-verbally. Here's an exploration of the power of active listening in family dynamics:

Building Trust: Active listening creates a foundation of trust within the family. When family members feel heard and understood, they are more likely to open up and share their thoughts, feelings, and concerns. Trust is a key element in healthy family relationships.

Fostering Empathy: Active listening encourages empathy, as it allows family members to step into each other's shoes and understand their perspectives and emotions. Empathy is essential for creating deeper connections and demonstrating care and support.

Conflict Resolution: Active listening is a valuable tool for resolving conflicts within the family. When family members actively listen to each other's concerns, it becomes easier to find common ground and work together toward solutions. It minimizes misunderstandings that often lead to disputes.

Promoting Open Communication: Actively listening to family members encourages open communication. When everyone feels that their voices are valued and respected, they are more likely to express their thoughts and feelings honestly and without fear of judgment.

Reducing Miscommunication: Active listening reduces the risk of miscommunication and misinterpretation. By clarifying what the speaker intends and asking for further information where necessary, family members can ensure they're on the same page.

Validation: Active listening provides a sense of validation. When family members listen actively, they signal that the speaker's thoughts and feelings are important. This validation boosts self-esteem and promotes a sense of self-worth.

Conflict Prevention: Actively listening to family members can also help prevent conflicts from arising in the first place. By addressing concerns and issues early on, families can maintain healthier relationships and prevent resentment from building.

Enhanced Problem Solving: Active listening is a critical part of effective problem-solving. Family members can collaborate more efficiently when they actively listen to each other's ideas, opinions, and suggestions.

Strengthening Bonds: The act of active listening deepens the emotional bonds within the family. It shows that family members genuinely care about each other's well-being and are willing to invest time and effort into understanding each other.

Modelling Behavior: Parents who actively listen to their children model the importance of this skill. Children learn valuable communication techniques by observing their parents' behaviour, which they can apply in their interactions.

In essence, active listening is a powerful tool for strengthening family relationships, enhancing understanding, and promoting effective communication. It requires patience, empathy, and a genuine interest in the thoughts and feelings of family members. By actively listening, families can create a supportive and harmonious environment where each member feels valued and heard.

Listening to others lets them know you are working to understand the message they are sending. You need to make sure that your body language conveys to them that you're interested and you're listening. You can make eye contact with them or turn your body towards them as they're talking. Whenever we go out and we are having dinner or lunch, my phone is usually on Do Not Disturb because I know that my phone can be a huge distraction. When I communicate with you, I am inside the conversation so I am interested.

Many of us have lost the ability to get into conversations. Communication involves connecting and many of us don't connect. There is no active listening without you connecting with who is speaking with you.

When you are listening actively, people know that you are listening to them, there are no distractions and you are focused on the message. When my children come to me and say "Mom do you have a minute?" The first thing I do is to drop my phone because I know that is a huge distraction then I say "Okay what are you saying?" sometimes what they are saying is not even something I want to listen to but believe me it makes all of the difference. Drop your phone the moment your child or your spouse is talking to you. In my home, there's a phone dropping time, when you come back from work, your phone is usually in one corner. You must pay attention to these things - gadgets so that it doesn't ruin the connection you are supposed to be building and try listening. I tell my children "Okay once I'm done with this reading, I will come and then we'll have the conversation" because I don't want to be distracted.

Active listening means listening for the content and the feelings behind the words. When you listen to me for instance, there are a lot of feelings behind the words that I speak. Everybody has feelings behind their words so when people are talking, don't just listen to what is being said, listen to the feeling that the person is trying to convey to you. Are they expressing joy, sadness, excitement, or anger, either through their words or body language? Sometimes people are speaking to us and they are not even saying the words but it's in the things that they don't say, if you listen, you hear it.

When you are listening attentively especially when you're not asked to advise, please do not offer, even to your children. The person first needs to know that you have understood them and their message is clear to you. Sometimes when you listen, the person is not asking you for advice. I have realized this a lot of the time so when my children are speaking, I'm listening to them. Sometimes your children just want you to be quiet, they just want an ear, sometimes your spouse does not want you to blame them when they're talking to you, they just want someone to listen and that's why I keep saying that discipline is not an emergency.

Your children come to you with things that they know are wrong and at that moment, trying to tell them what they are doing is wrong, you have shut them down and they are no longer listening. I remember when our son came home from a particular game that he knows is not allowed in our home because it's online. Of course, they've gone to school and people have talked about it so he wanted to play and he said "Mommy I was so pushed to come home and try this game so that I can join in the conversation."

While he was saying it, I said "Do you want to try it?" It was not a time to advise. I didn't need to come and start preaching to him of our family values, he already knows all that and I know that he knew at that time that what he needed was wisdom. He decided on his own a day after that conversation that it wasn't necessary just because I could connect with him.

Sometimes your children just want you to listen, you can correct a child without saying a word and that's effective communication. Sometimes your child just wants wisdom not instruction, your child just wants you to know or hear. If you share wisdom, your children will fight with you less. The reason there is so much fight and argument is that your children do not see you sharing wisdom. Instructions are not the same as wisdom, sometimes the only thing that your child needs is wisdom and active listening. You are going to be very surprised how your conversations and relationship will change when you focus on listening to the other person, rather than thinking of your next response. Leave your response alone, you will have your day that's why we have family meetings in our homes where you can have your day.

TOOL 2: NON VERBAL COMMUNICATION

Non-verbal communication plays a significant role in conveying messages, feelings, and intentions within the family. It complements verbal communication and can sometimes be more powerful in expressing emotions and thoughts. Here's an exploration of how non-verbal communication tools, such as body language, facial expressions, gestures, posture, and tone of voice, contribute to effective communication in family dynamics, along with examples:

Understanding Body Language:
Example 1 - Open Arms and Relaxed Posture: When a family member welcomes another with open arms and a relaxed posture, it signals warmth and acceptance. This body language communicates that they are approachable and ready for a positive interaction.

Example 2 - Crossed Arms and Frowning: Conversely, crossed arms and a frowning expression can indicate defensiveness or displeasure. In a family context, if a teenager uses this body language when discussing a family issue, it may suggest resistance or discomfort.

The Impact of Facial Expressions:
Example 1 - Smiles and Eye Contact: A genuine smile and maintaining eye contact during a family conversation convey warmth and attentiveness. It indicates interest and positive engagement in the discussion.

Example 2 - Raised Eyebrows and Furrowed Forehead: Raised eyebrows and a furrowed forehead can signal confusion or concern. If a family member uses these expressions during a discussion about a plan, it may indicate their need for clarification or their apprehensions.

Gestures, Posture, and Tone of Voice:

Example 1 - Nodding and Leaning Forward: Nodding in agreement and leaning forward in a conversation with a family member demonstrates active engagement. These gestures, combined with a friendly tone of voice, show support and interest in their words.

Example 2 - Arms Crossed and Defensive Tone: If a family member crosses their arms and uses a defensive tone when discussing a sensitive topic like finances, it suggests that they may be feeling guarded or anxious about the conversation.

Example 3 - Slouched Posture and Monotone Voice: A slouched posture and a monotone voice can convey boredom or disinterest. For instance, if a family member adopts these non-verbal cues during a discussion about future goals, it may indicate that they are not fully engaged in the topic.

Non-verbal communication is a powerful tool because it often reveals genuine emotions and intentions. Family members can use these cues to better understand each other's feelings, needs, and reactions. To enhance effective communication within the family, it's important for all members to be mindful of their non-verbal communication and to be perceptive of the non-verbal cues displayed by others. This awareness can lead to improved understanding and more harmonious family interactions.

TOOL 3: "I STATEMENTS"

"I statements" are a valuable communication tool that can have a significant impact on problem-solving within the family. They provide a structured and constructive way to express feelings, thoughts, and concerns while minimizing blame and defensiveness. Here's how "I statements" can influence problem-solving in the family:

Ownership of Feelings and Needs: "I statements" start with the word "I," which indicates ownership of the speaker's feelings and needs. By taking responsibility for their emotions, family members communicate that they are sharing their perspectives rather than assigning blame to others. This reduces defensiveness and fosters a more open dialogue.

Example: "I feel overwhelmed when there's a lot of clutter in our shared spaces, and I need a clean and organized environment to relax."

Clarification and Understanding: "I statements" encourage clear and specific communication. When a family member uses an "I statement," it offers clarity about their emotions and the reasons behind them. This enables other family members to better understand what is bothering them, which is crucial for effective problem-solving.

Example: "I feel frustrated when we don't stick to our agreed-upon schedule for family outings because it makes planning my day difficult."

Reduced Defensiveness: By avoiding blame and focusing on their feelings and needs, "I statements" reduce the likelihood of defensive reactions from others. Family members are more likely to respond with empathy and a willingness to address the concerns expressed.

Example: "I feel hurt when I perceive criticism in your comments about my choices, and I would appreciate it if we could discuss our differences in a more supportive way."

Encouragement of Empathy: "I statements" encourage empathy and active listening. When one family member uses an "I statement," it invites the others to listen to their feelings and needs, which can lead to greater understanding and compassion.

Example: "I feel anxious when we argue about household chores, and I need us to find a fair and balanced way to share responsibilities."

Problem Identification and Resolution: "I statements" facilitate the identification of specific problems or issues within the family. When each family member expresses their concerns using "I statements," it helps pinpoint the root causes of conflicts, making it easier to work together to find solutions.

Example: "I feel concerned when we overspend our budget, and I think we should create a family financial plan to address this issue."

Enhanced Communication Skills: Encouraging the use of "I statements" within the family promotes effective communication skills. Family members learn to express themselves assertively while respecting the feelings and needs of others, leading to healthier and more productive discussions.

In summary, "I statements" are a powerful communication tool in family dynamics, as they allow family members to express themselves honestly while minimizing blame and defensiveness. When used effectively, they can foster empathy, clarity, and problem-solving, creating a more harmonious and understanding family environment. Encouraging the practice of "I statements" can lead to improved communication and conflict resolution within the family.

TOOL 4: CONFLICT RESOLUTION:

Conflict resolution is a crucial tool for solving family problems and maintaining healthy relationships within the family. Teaching your children effective conflict resolution skills is a valuable life lesson. Here's how to use conflict resolution as a tool in solving family problems, along with examples of how to practice it and teach it to your children:

Teaching Conflict Resolution: Model Healthy Conflict Resolution: Children learn by example. Demonstrate healthy conflict resolution in your interactions with family members. Show them how to listen actively, express their feelings assertively, and work together to find solutions.

- Open Communication: Encourage open communication within the family. Teach your children that it's okay to express their feelings and concerns. Create an environment where everyone feels comfortable sharing their thoughts and emotions.
- Active Listening: Teach your children the importance of active listening. Explain that listening attentively to what others have to say is a crucial part of conflict resolution. Encourage them to ask questions for clarity and understanding.
- Expressing Feelings: Help your children express their feelings and needs using "I statement." Encourage them to say how they feel and what they need or want when conflicts arise.

Practicing Conflict Resolution:

Conflict Timeouts: Teach your children the concept of taking a "conflict timeout" when emotions run high. Explain that stepping away from the situation temporarily to cool off and gather thoughts can lead to more productive discussions.

- Problem-Solving Discussions: Engage your children in problem-solving discussions. When conflicts arise, gather together as a family to discuss the issue calmly and rationally. Encourage brainstorming solutions and compromises.
- Apologize and Forgive: Teach your children that it's okay to apologise when they make a mistake or hurt someone's feelings. Encourage them to say "I'm sorry" when necessary and to practise forgiveness when others apologise.
- Use Visual Aids: For younger children, visual aids like a "conflict resolution chart" can be helpful. Create a simple chart with steps such as "Listen," "Express Feelings," "Brainstorm Solutions," and "Agree on a Solution." This provides a visual guide for resolving conflicts.

Examples of Conflict Resolution in Family Practice

Example 1: If two siblings are arguing over a shared toy, encourage them to sit down and discuss the issue. Teach them to express their feelings using "I statements" and work together to find a solution, such as taking turns playing with the toy.

Example 2: When a teenager and a parent disagree about curfew, hold a family meeting to discuss the issue. Encourage both parties to express their concerns and needs. Work together to establish a curfew that both parties can agree on.

Example 3: If siblings are arguing over chores, gather the family for a discussion. Encourage them to brainstorm ways to divide chores fairly and create a chore chart that outlines each family member's responsibilities.

Example 4: In the event of a family misunderstanding, such as miscommunication about a family event, gather together and discuss what happened. Encourage open communication, apologize for any confusion, and find ways to prevent similar misunderstandings in the future.

Teaching and practicing conflict resolution within the family helps children develop essential life skills that can benefit them in various situations. It also fosters a harmonious family environment where conflicts are addressed constructively and with respect for one another.

TOOL 5: "WE" LANGUAGE

"We" language is a powerful communication tool that emphasizes unity and shared responsibility within the family. By framing discussions and problem-solving efforts using "we" language, family members can address issues collaboratively and foster a sense of togetherness. Here's how to use "we" language as a tool in resolving family issues:

Emphasizing Collective Responsibility: When addressing family issues, encourage the use of "we" language to emphasize that challenges and solutions are shared responsibilities. This approach promotes a sense of unity and teamwork.

Example: Instead of saying, "You need to clean your room," say, "We need to work together to keep our living space clean."

Promoting Collaboration:
"We" language encourages family members to collaborate on finding solutions to problems. It reinforces the idea that everyone has a role to play in resolving issues and achieving common goals.
Example: Instead of saying, "You need to do the dishes," say, "Can we all pitch in to do the dishes after dinner?"

Fostering Empathy: Using "we" language allows family members to consider the perspectives and needs of others. It promotes empathy by signaling that everyone's well-being and opinions matter.
Example: Instead of saying, "You never consider my feelings," say, "Let's discuss how we can both address our feelings and concerns."

Sharing Ownership of Solutions: When resolving family issues, "we" language encourages all family members to share ownership of the solutions. It reinforces the idea that working together leads to better outcomes.
Example: Instead of saying, "You should find a solution to this problem," say, "Let's brainstorm and find a solution that works for all of us."

Strengthening Family Bonds: "We" language helps strengthen family bonds by highlighting that family members are a team, supporting and caring for one another. It promotes a sense of belonging and togetherness.
Example: Instead of saying, "Your actions are causing problems," say, "We can overcome these challenges together if we work as a team."

Encouraging Inclusive Decision-Making: In family problem-solving, "we" language encourages inclusive decision-making. It communicates that family members have an equal say in finding solutions and resolving issues.
Example: Instead of saying, "I've made a decision," say, "Let's all discuss and make a decision together."

Maintaining Positive Communication: "We" language contributes to positive and collaborative communication within the family. It sets a tone that encourages open and constructive discussions.
Example: Instead of saying, "You're causing conflicts," say, "Let's talk about how we can prevent conflicts in the future."

Celebrating Achievements Together: "We" language is not limited to problem-solving; it can also be used to celebrate achievements and milestones as a family. It reinforces the idea that success is a shared experience.
Example: Instead of saying, "I did it," say, "We accomplished this together, and I'm proud of our teamwork."
By using "we" language as a tool in resolving family issues, family members can work together to address challenges, build stronger bonds, and maintain a harmonious family environment. It promotes a sense of unity and shared responsibility, which is essential for effective problem-solving and mutual support within the family.

TOOL 6: EMPATHY AND VALIDATION

Empathy and validation are powerful tools for solving family problems, fostering understanding, and maintaining healthy relationships. Here's how these tools can be used effectively within the family context:
- Empathy:
- Understanding Emotions: Encourage family members to understand and acknowledge each other's emotions. Empathy involves recognizing and validating the feelings and perspectives of others.
- Active Listening: Teach family members to actively listen to one another during discussions. This means giving their full attention, avoiding interruptions, and responding with empathy to what is being said.

- Seeing from Others' Perspectives: Promote the idea that everyone in the family has a unique perspective and experiences. Encourage family members to put themselves in each other's shoes to understand their viewpoints.
  Example: If one family member is upset about a recent move, encourage the others to empathize by saying, "I can understand how this change is affecting you. It's a big adjustment."
- Support During Tough Times: Emphasize the importance of offering support and comfort to family members during difficult moments. Let them know that their feelings are valid and that they are not alone in their struggles.
- Validation:
- Acknowledging Feelings: Validation involves acknowledging and accepting the feelings of family members. It means recognizing that their emotions are real and legitimate, even if you don't necessarily share the same perspective.
- Respect for Individual Experiences: Stress the importance of respecting each family member's unique experiences and emotions. Validation reassures them that their feelings matter.
- Problem-Solving from a Supportive Foundation: When family members feel validated, they are more likely to engage in problem-solving from a supportive and understanding foundation. They will be open to finding solutions that consider everyone's needs.
  Example: If a family member is worried about a job interview, validate their feelings by saying, "I understand how important this is to you, and I believe in your abilities. We're here to support you in any way we can."
- Conflict Resolution: Validation can be a key component of conflict resolution. When family members feel heard and validated, they are more willing to collaborate and find common ground.
- Promoting Self-Esteem: Validation can boost the self-esteem and self-worth of family members. When their feelings are validated, they are more likely to have a positive self-image.

Using empathy and validation as tools in family problem-solving involves creating an environment of trust, understanding, and support. These tools can help family members feel valued and heard, which, in turn, can lead to more effective communication, collaboration, and resolution of issues. By teaching and practicing empathy and validation, families can build stronger bonds and navigate challenges more effectively.

TOOL 7: OPEN ENDED QUESTIONS

Open-ended questions are a powerful tool in solving family problems because they encourage in-depth discussions, foster understanding, and promote collaborative problem-solving. Here's how to effectively use open-ended questions within the family context:
Encouraging Thoughtful Responses:
Use open-ended questions to prompt family members to think deeply about the issue at hand. These questions cannot be answered with a simple "yes" or "no," encouraging individuals to provide more detailed and thoughtful responses.
Example: Instead of asking, "Did you have a good day?" ask, "What was the most exciting or challenging part of your day?"

- Promoting Active Listening:
  Open-ended questions invite family members to share their thoughts and feelings. When family members use open-ended questions, it's essential to actively listen to one another's responses, demonstrating that their perspectives are valued.
  Example: In response to a family member sharing their challenges, ask, "How did that make you feel? What can we do to support you?"
- Exploring Different Perspectives:
  Open-ended questions encourage the exploration of different viewpoints and experiences. They create space for family members to share their thoughts and emotions, which can lead to a deeper understanding of the issue and those involved.

Example: When discussing a family conflict, ask, "What are your thoughts on how we can resolve this situation? How do you think it has affected each of us?"

- Problem Identification and Resolution:
Use open-ended questions to delve into the root causes of family problems. These questions can help identify the underlying issues and concerns, paving the way for effective problem-solving.
Example: To address a recurring family issue, ask, "What do you think is the main challenge here? How can we work together to find a solution?"

- Encouraging Collaboration:
Open-ended questions create a collaborative atmosphere by involving family members in the problem-solving process. Everyone has an opportunity to contribute their ideas and perspectives.
Example: In a discussion about family goals, ask, "What goals do we want to achieve together as a family? How can each of us contribute to these goals?"

- Promoting Reflection:
Open-ended questions encourage family members to reflect on their feelings, behaviours, and potential solutions. This reflection can lead to personal growth and a more profound awareness of how their actions impact the family.
Example: After a family disagreement, ask, "What have we learned from this experience? How can we avoid similar conflicts in the future?"

Using open-ended questions as a tool in family problem-solving allows family members to engage in deeper, more meaningful discussions. It promotes active participation, empathy, and collaboration, leading to a more thorough understanding of issues and effective solutions. Encouraging the use of open-ended questions in family communication can help create a supportive and harmonious environment where problems are addressed constructively.

TOOL 8: FAMILY MEETING

Family meetings are a valuable tool for resolving family problems and fostering open communication. These meetings provide a structured and consistent way to address issues, discuss concerns, and work together as a family to find solutions. Here's how to start and use family meetings effectively:

1. Setting the Stage: Schedule Regular Meetings: Choose a specific day and time for family meetings, making them a regular part of your family's routine. Consistency is key to ensuring everyone can plan to attend.
Create a Safe and Supportive Space: Find a comfortable and quiet place for the meetings. Make it clear that family meetings are a judgment-free zone where everyone can express themselves.

2. Preparing for Family Meetings: Agenda: Encourage family members to contribute to the meeting agenda. Each family member can suggest topics they'd like to discuss during the meeting. Having an agenda ensures that important issues are addressed.
Roles: Consider assigning roles for the meetings, such as a facilitator (perhaps a parent), a timekeeper, and a note-taker. These roles help keep the meeting organized and on track.

3. Conducting Family Meetings: Start with Positives: Begin each meeting by sharing positive experiences or achievements. This sets a positive tone and reminds everyone of their strengths.
Discuss Concerns: Address any concerns or issues that family members have added to the agenda. Encourage open and respectful communication. Use active listening to ensure everyone feels heard.
Brainstorm Solutions: When discussing problems, encourage family members to brainstorm solutions together. This collaborative approach allows family members to participate in finding resolutions.
Set Goals: As a family, set achievable goals based on the issues discussed. Create a plan for how you'll work together to reach these goals.

4. Practicing Effective Communication: Active Listening: Emphasize the importance of active listening during family meetings. Encourage family members to focus on the speaker, avoid interruptions, and ask clarifying questions when needed.
I Statements: Teach family members to use "I statements" when expressing their feelings and concerns. This helps prevent blame and fosters understanding.

5. Celebrating Achievements: At the end of each meeting, take a moment to celebrate achievements, no matter how small. This reinforces positive behaviour and encourages continued progress.

6. Consistent Follow-Up: After family meetings, it's important to follow up on the goals and action plans that were set during the meeting. This reinforces the commitment to finding solutions and making improvements.

7. Adjust and Adapt: Family meetings can evolve as needed. If certain aspects of the meetings are not working well or if the family's needs change, be open to adjusting the format and structure.
Family meetings are a tool for creating a safe and open space where family members can express themselves, address problems, and work collaboratively to find solutions. By implementing regular family meetings, you can strengthen communication, build trust, and resolve family problems more effectively.

TOOL 9: APOLOGY AND FORGIVENESS:

Apology and Forgiveness: Tools for Resolving Family Issues. Apology and forgiveness are powerful tools for resolving family issues and mending relationships. They help in acknowledging mistakes, healing emotional wounds, and rebuilding trust. Here's how to use these tools effectively within the family context:

- Apology:
- Recognize the Impact: Teach family members to recognize the impact of their actions and words on others. It's essential to understand how behaviour has affected the family members who were hurt.
- Sincere Apology: Encourage those who have caused harm to offer a sincere apology. This involves taking responsibility for their actions and expressing genuine remorse.
- "I'm Sorry": Emphasize the importance of saying "I'm sorry." Teach family members to use this phrase when apologizing for their behaviour.
- Make Amends: Encourage those who have caused harm to make amends for their actions. This may involve taking steps to rectify the situation or make things right.
- Commit to Change: Apologies should be followed by a commitment to change. Family members should express their intention to avoid repeating the same behaviour in the future.
- Forgiveness:
- Understanding Forgiveness: Teach family members what forgiveness means. It doesn't mean forgetting or condoning the hurtful behaviour, but it does mean letting go of the anger and resentment associated with it.
- Empathy: Promote empathy by encouraging family members to try to understand the perspective of the person who hurt them. This can help in the forgiveness process.
- Express Forgiveness: Encourage family members to express their forgiveness. This can be done through words or actions that demonstrate a willingness to move past the hurt.
- Letting Go of Resentment: Stress the importance of letting go of resentment and grudges. Holding onto negative emotions can harm family relationships.
- Rebuilding Trust: Forgiveness is a step toward rebuilding trust. Family members should understand that trust may take time to fully restore.

Apology and Forgiveness in Practice: Example 1: If a family member was hurt by harsh words during an argument, the offending family member can apologize by saying, "I'm sorry for the hurtful things I said. I was wrong, and I regret it."

Example 2: The offended family member can express forgiveness by saying, "I forgive you for what you said. I hope we can move forward and communicate better in the future."

Example 3: In a situation where one family member broke another's trust by sharing a secret, the offending family member can apologize by saying, "I apologize for breaking your trust. I understand how much it hurt you."

Example 4: The offended family member can express forgiveness by saying, "I forgive you for what happened, but it will take some time for me to fully trust you again."

Using apologies and forgiveness as tools within the family context allows family members to heal and move forward after conflicts and hurtful situations. These tools promote understanding, empathy, and the rebuilding of trust, ultimately strengthening family relationships and facilitating problem resolution.

share more on understanding the apology language of each family member and how it impacts solving problems

Understanding Apology Language in the Family

Just as people have unique love languages, they also have distinct apology languages. Apology languages describe how individuals prefer to receive apologies and, conversely, how they tend to apologize to others. Understanding the apology languages of family members can significantly impact problem-solving and conflict resolution within the family. Here are the five apology languages, along with their characteristics and how they influence problem-solving:

1. Expressing Regret:

Characteristics: People with this apology language express regret by saying, "I'm sorry" and acknowledging their actions were wrong.

Impact on Problem-Solving: Family members with this language value heartfelt apologies. They need to hear "I'm sorry" and genuine remorse to feel that the issue is being addressed.

2. Accepting Responsibility:

Characteristics: This apology language involves taking responsibility for one's actions, admitting fault, and accepting the consequences.

Impact on Problem-Solving: Family members with this language appreciate when the responsible party owns up to their actions. Accepting responsibility is crucial for resolving issues.

3. Making Restitution:

Characteristics: People with this language want to make amends and compensate for their wrongdoings through actions or reparations.

Impact on Problem-Solving: In family conflicts, those with this apology language prefer to see concrete efforts to make things right. They feel that actions speak louder than words.

4. Genuinely Repenting:

Characteristics: Genuinely repentant individuals show a commitment to change their behaviour and avoid repeating the same mistakes.

Impact on Problem-Solving: Family members with this apology language value not only an apology but also a sincere intention to change. They expect that the problem won't recur.

5. Requesting Forgiveness:

Characteristics: Those with this apology language explicitly ask for forgiveness as part of their apology.

Impact on Problem-Solving: Family members with this language often need to hear the words "Will you forgive me?" They feel that forgiveness is a necessary step in resolving the issue.

Understanding each family member's apology language is vital because it helps tailor apologies to what they need to hear and experience. Here's how it impacts problem-solving:

- More Effective Apologies: When family members use apology language that resonates with the recipient, the apologies are more effective. This can lead to quicker resolution of issues.
- Improved Communication: Understanding apology languages can improve communication within the family. Family members

can express their apologies in a way that's better received, reducing misunderstandings.

- Greater Empathy: Recognizing each other's apology language fosters empathy. It helps family members understand each other's needs and perspectives.
- Conflict Resolution: When family members feel heard and understood through their preferred apology language, it's easier to move toward conflict resolution. Apologies become a bridge to problem-solving.
- Rebuilding Trust: Apologizing in the right way can aid in rebuilding trust. Family members who know their apology language are being considered are more likely to trust the sincerity of the apologies.

By understanding and respecting each family member's apology language, you can create a more harmonious and supportive family environment where apologies are not just words but meaningful steps toward resolving conflicts and maintaining strong relationships.

TOOL 10: AVOIDING BLAME AND CRITICISM

Avoiding blame and criticism is a crucial tool for resolving conflicts within the family. Blame and criticism can escalate conflicts, damage relationships, and hinder productive problem-solving. Here's how to use this tool effectively:

1. Recognize the Harm of Blame and Criticism: Understand that blame and criticism can be damaging. They often lead to defensiveness, resentment, and a communication breakdown.

2. Promote Responsibility and Accountability: Encourage family members to take responsibility for their actions and words. When addressing conflicts, start by acknowledging one's role in the situation.

Stress that taking responsibility does not mean accepting blame but rather recognizing how one's actions contributed to the issue.

3. Use "I Statements" and Assertive Communication: Teach family members to use "I statements" when expressing their feelings and concerns. This approach focuses on personal experiences and emotions without blaming others.
Promote assertive communication, where family members can express themselves confidently and respectfully without resorting to blame or criticism.

4. Encourage Open Communication: Create an environment where open and honest communication is encouraged. Family members should feel safe sharing their thoughts, concerns, and emotions without fear of criticism or blame.

5. Practice Empathy: Encourage family members to practice empathy by trying to understand the perspectives and feelings of others. This can lead to more compassionate and understanding discussions.

6. Focus on the Issue, Not the Person: Stress that conflicts should be about addressing the issue at hand, not attacking or blaming the person. Encourage family members to discuss the problem without resorting to personal attacks.

7. Collaborative Problem-Solving: Promote a problem-solving approach to conflicts. Encourage family members to work together to find solutions rather than pointing fingers or placing blame.

8. Take a Time-Out When Needed: Teach family members that it's okay to take a time-out when emotions run high. Stepping away from a conflict temporarily to cool off and gather thoughts can prevent the escalation of blame and criticism.

9. Encourage Feedback and Reflection: After conflicts are resolved, encourage family members to provide feedback on how the communication can be improved. Reflection and learning from past conflicts can lead to more effective future discussions.

10. Reinforce Positive Communication Habits: Celebrate and reinforce positive communication habits within the family. When family members engage in constructive, blame-free communication, acknowledge and appreciate their efforts.

11. Seek Mediation if Necessary: If conflicts within the family persist and cannot be resolved internally, consider seeking external mediation from a professional, such as a family therapist or counsellor, to facilitate productive discussions.

By avoiding blame and criticism, family members can foster healthier communication, resolve conflicts more effectively, and strengthen their relationships. This tool creates a more supportive and understanding family environment where issues are addressed constructively, leading to more harmonious relationships.

TOOL 11: SETTING BOUNDARIES

Setting boundaries is a powerful tool for resolving family problems. Boundaries help family members establish clear expectations, maintain individual autonomy, and create a harmonious and respectful environment. Here's how to use this tool effectively:

1. Understand the Purpose of Boundaries: Recognize that boundaries are not about creating distance or disconnection within the family but about defining personal space and respecting each other's needs.

2. Open Communication: Promote open and honest communication about boundaries. Encourage family members to discuss their needs, preferences, and comfort zones with one another.

3. Identify Individual Boundaries: Encourage each family member to identify and express their boundaries. This includes areas related to personal space, privacy, emotional needs, and personal time.

4. Respect Each Other's Boundaries: Stress the importance of respecting and honouring the boundaries set by family members. Emphasize that boundaries are valid, and everyone deserves to have their limits respected.

5. Discuss and Set Family Boundaries: Encourage the family as a whole to discuss and set boundaries that apply to the entire household. This could include rules related to shared spaces, responsibilities, and schedules.

6. Adjust Boundaries as Needed: Highlight that boundaries can change over time and should be adjusted when necessary. Family members should feel comfortable revisiting and modifying their boundaries as their needs evolve.

7. Communicate Consequences: When setting boundaries, it's important to communicate the consequences of violating them. This helps maintain accountability and respect for each other's limits.

8. Be Flexible and Compromise: Teach family members to be flexible and willing to compromise. Sometimes, boundaries may conflict, so it's important to find solutions that respect everyone's needs.

9. Use "I Statements" for Boundary Setting:
Encourage the use of "I statements" when expressing the need for a boundary. For example, say, "I need some alone time in the evening" rather than "You need to leave me alone in the evening."

10. Set Technology Boundaries: Discuss and establish boundaries related to technology use within the family. This includes screen time limits, appropriate content, and respect for technology-free times (e.g., during family meals).

11. Promote Self-Care: Emphasize the importance of self-care as a boundary-setting tool. Encourage family members to prioritize self-care and communicate their needs for self-care time.

12. Respect the Boundaries of Others: Teach family members to be mindful of each other's boundaries. Show that respecting boundaries is a sign of love and consideration.

13. Seek Professional Help If Necessary: If family problems persist or if there is difficulty in establishing and respecting boundaries, consider seeking assistance from a family therapist or counsellor to facilitate discussions and resolution.

Setting boundaries within the family creates a framework for mutual respect, understanding, and problem-solving. It helps prevent conflicts and misunderstandings by clearly defining what is acceptable and respectful behavior. This tool fosters an environment of harmony, where family members can coexist while respecting each other's individuality and needs.

By incorporating these communication tools into your family interactions, you can create an atmosphere of understanding, empathy, and cooperation, which is essential for building and maintaining a strong family

HOW DO YOU TEACH YOUR CHILDREN TO COMMUNICATE?

children have to learn to express themselves clearly and how to listen to others as well. if the communication in the home must become effective then you must teach your children intentionally how to communicate from the moment your child begins to alter the first sound.

They are learning how to communicate so whether you teach it intentionally or unintentionally, your children are going to learn something whether they learn it ineffectively or effectively, they are learning how to get attention from others, how to get their message across they're learning that communication is a two-way process, they learn their skills from how you respond to them and how you communicate with them.

Many parents come to me and say my children are always yelling, I don't know how to help my children but when you look at it, you find out that for those that are in that home, the only language they understand is actually how to yell.

"Parenting is first about you", this is to me the most profound quote in my book 'Connect to Correct'. Parenting is first about you and if you make it about your child then you miss the mark which is the very problem. If you have a home that is full of aggression, you will build a communication language of aggression. If your home is filled with love, peace and understanding, you will equally build a similar communication language.

Here are pointers you must note in actively teaching your children effective communication

Communication starts with you even when your child is zero, one of the first steps in teaching our children to listen actively to them. When we are actively listening to our children, we are letting them know that they can send their message and their message is important to us as noted.

Give them your full attention listening for feelings as well as the content. We must refrain from offering advice when we are listening even to our children for us to understand.

Actively teach your children how to listen. The child needs to focus on the person who is talking eliminating any distractions just as we give them our attention you need to also teach them how to give

attention to others to be sure that they've understood your message.
Ask them to repeat back in their own words what they hear from you.

Children can also be asked what feelings they are picking up from you when you communicate, this will help build their emotional intelligence, I share how to build your child's emotions in my book RAISING THE EMOTIONALLY INTELLIGENT CHILD. We often ask our children "What could you read from the content of my talk?" If the child does not repeat the message clearly, that offers you time for clarification and another opportunity to teach effective communication.

Children learn mostly by communicating with us and by watching how others communicate with each other. So, how you are communicating with your spouse becomes a curriculum for them. Your children are picking up your communication culture and it will eventually become their norm. We need to be good role models and to take time to listen, as well as listen to our message.

Families must establish good lines of communication so that all family members can be heard and understood.

Compromise does not mean that there's a winner and a loser but generates a win-win solution; it challenges us to be creative in developing solutions to problems rather than just focusing on our own needs. So what we do in my home is that we come up with a win-win solution so family members need good communication skills so that everybody's point of view and suggestions will be expressed clearly and ahead by the other family members.

Here are some of the ways that we come up with a win-win solution in my own home
All persons experiencing conflict must be included even if it means a 10-minute timeout so that people can calm down.

Use neutral language. This means that family members are not allowed to name call or pass judgment on others' ideas or needs, each person's request needs to be considered, each opinion needs to be heard, and everybody needs to use their active listening skills.

Once everybody feels heard and understood then the process can move to generating new solutions to resolve conflict.

Step by step to solving challenges through effective communication

- Starting the discussion: the first step in resolving any challenge through effective communication is to start the discussion. Wait until you're not angry to discuss the problem. Family problems can be very painful, if your family members are arguing, waiting until everybody's calm can help keep the argument from escalating into a full-blown issue.

- Apply the power of initial nothing. Many times we're in a hurry. When people are arguing, that's not the time amid the moment to try and solve the issue. One of the things you want to learn to do is to step back and wait when there is a conflict. Waiting allows you to approach the issues logically I need you to imbibe the power of initial nothing in solving family problems

- When there is conflict, restrain from trying to make a big deal, from trying to prove a point. Even if with a child, you must understand that is not an emergency. it allows you to approach it logically rather than emotionally. if you take a step back and give yourself some time to think before dealing with that issue you won't deal with it so reactively. Approaching someone when they are angry will heighten the intensity. An angry child is not a listening child.

- Apply emotional control. When you master your emotions you are a winner because everything won't be about you. Emotions control is key to effective communication.

- Deal with family problems in person preferably. Try as much as possible to deal with family problems in person.

- Keep your language positive when you talk to your family. Avoid language that blames any member of the family, or that feels negative. Negativity is a vicious cycle, don't find yourself there. Keeping your language positive means avoiding judgmental words, or name-calling of any family member, it means avoiding accusatory words that are said in an angry tone.

- Avoid the need to win the argument about the problem. It's not all about winning the argument, it is about being able to develop a plan for solving problems together.

- Focus on organizing activities that can be fun together, and avoid anything that could serve as a trigger in reigniting the problem. Keep your tone and your voice calm, let it be modulated. If you cannot, if you're in a place where you know that you are going to get triggered or your voice is going to rise, please step away from that place and attempt to calm down before engaging in the conversation.

- Forgive any family member who has wronged you. This can be very difficult to achieve as it's not very easy to forgive the person, family member or not, whom we think has wronged us. However, ultimately, forgiveness is about freeing yourself from the corrosive level of the nature of the dispute. Forgiving family members is about letting go of the past so you can build a healthier future.

- Figure out the problem. Resolving a problem is in understanding the root of the problem. Most times what we think the problem is, might not even be the problem. Always ask, "What is the root cause of this problem?" "Why did this happen?" "Why is my child misbehaving?" Sometimes you might even need to engage in self-analysis, "Why am I hiding this issue?" "Why am I afraid of bringing it up?" You'll find that the problem may even be you, could be past trauma.

- The need to diagnose the exact problem cannot be over-emphasized. Ask questions; a good technique for actually digging out the root cause of family problems. Ask questions rather than making statements that make people feel judged. And they end up putting up a defense. We do that a lot with our children, we put them in situations where they have no option but to lie to us. They will lie to you there's nothing you can do about it. It's not about raising them well or not because lying is instinctive. That's one of the ways the brain saves itself. You put them in a situation, you set them up for failure as though you are waiting for them to make mistakes, instead of teaching them what they should do. You buy canes and then you're waiting for your child to make a mistake you now bring out the cane as if to say I'm waiting for you.

- Ask relevant questions, not questions to pressure. Make the questions open-ended so that you elicit more elaborate responses. Listen attentively because you might be solving the problem while you're doing that. Open a line of communication.

- Avoid gossiping about other people as a family. When you talk about your child in front of another child, what is done to one is done to all, you create a system in your home that talks about people behind their backs.

A parent reached out to me once and in her words, "Coach I messed up. My son did something and lied to me so I was triggered and I started to scream everywhere. I didn't know that what I had done to my son had an impact on my daughter. One week later something else happened and my daughter lied. This is my daughter who would never lie. I called her to find out what was happening and she said, because of how I reacted when her brother made a mistake, she didn't want me to react that way."

What is done to one is done to all. Your children hear you on the phone complain about one child to one sister or one friend. You need to be careful because that can be the root of the problem.

- Try to reach a compromise. Compromise does not mean that you are trying to take sides, it means that you come up with solutions that both can feel okay about even when it's neither exactly what they want. A compromise is a good way to diffuse a dispute or to address a family problem. Think about compromise as the first step to trying to figure out whether a problem is solvable, depending on its nature. What is already being done to solve the issue? If you've tried and tried and keep getting the same result that may be different, but consider what points of common ground you can have. You don't have to give in to everything. One technique for reaching a compromise is for both people in the dispute to sit down and draw up two circles that relate to the problem. In the first circle, write out everything you are willing to compromise on. In the other circle, write the areas you're willing to bend and then share the circles which is very important.

- Take the family members one-on-one: talk to them one-on-one. Some families don't function well as a group. You must understand your family dynamics so that in trying to practice all that you've learned you don't mess things up. You might want to talk to every family member one-on-one, and reach a compromise before you can now come together because if you do that and you have a dysfunctional family you might make a mess of the things that you have even started doing.

Please ensure that you understand your family Dynamics.

- Hold family meetings: If your home gets used to having a family meeting to discuss progress, you will find out that it's the best bet if a problem affects the entire family. In our home at the family meetings, we'll say "Okay things happen, can we talk about it?" Family meetings are an amazing place to study.

- Write letters to the family member: Handwritten letters will go a long way. In my own home, we write letters, my children are always writing letters to us, and we are always writing letters to them. Sometimes it's a letter to just say "I'm sorry". Handwritten is good because it's more personal, it shows that you put care and thought behind it and it seems warmer. It may make the family member realize that you are trying your best. Write them a letter about this issue that you've been battling with, and convey it in such a way that you're sincerely writing it for a transformational family, not for a transactional family. In that letter, you should explain how you feel and why you want to address the issue. Use the word "I" more than "you" in the letter so you're stating your perspective, not blaming or speaking for anyone. Explain how the problem is affecting you, how you would like the problem to be resolved and why this is a very important letter. When you are resolving this issue, if your children are the source of the family problem, whether it's acting disrespectful, arguing with siblings, or not doing their chores, you may want to deal with this issue a little differently if the child is wrong. Explain the problem clearly. You might want to say something like, "I've noticed that you don't get out of bed easily", or "we have noticed that you don't keep the time and we need to solve this". Don't get angry, instead ask the child how you can help in solving the problem. What I do with my children is that I suggest that they come up with a plan so that we can solve a problem. Give the child positive reinforcement as they make progress, and try to dig out the real reasons for the problem. Is it because the child is not sleeping well? Is the child on social media? Sometimes your child is up in the night but you don't even know.

- Letting go of family problems that's step four of solving family problems. Through effective communication establish boundaries. If your family members are toxic and they are causing harm to you and constant drama, there's nothing wrong with drawing boundaries and setting limits. This can be a healthy thing to do. If you have an abusive spouse, giving them space might be a good idea. If it's your child, you can put your food down, you can establish boundaries. You need to know when it's time to step back, there are family problems that take time to solve please do not be in a hurry to solve them, don't get yourself consumed. If it's a problem of substance use, for instance, you need to get help for the person it's not something you can do yourself you need a professional.

SEEK HELP

Some family problems are so deeply felt and toxic that they can only be solved by professionals, there's nothing to be ashamed of. Seek help, a family problem is rooted in trauma, substance abuse, mental illness and all of that. A professional will be your only way out. Many times we are dealing with childhood trauma that is so bad, that if you don't get a professional to dig deep into it, it will continue. There's nothing to be ashamed of about seeking help, it is very important.

Are your family relationships suffering because you argue over many things? Are family members staying away from, or ignoring each other? Are family members constantly seeking attention from people outside the family to fill the voids that they feel?

If you answered yes to any of the questions, it may be a wise decision to begin to seek family counselling immediately so that you don't break down that whole system.

A breakdown in family communication is a breakdown of the family itself, the family dies once the whole fabric of the communication is dead.

CHAPTER 6

DEALING WITH SPECIFIC FAMILY ISSUES

Dealing with specific family issues requires a tailored approach that considers the unique nature of each problem. Here are common family issues and strategies for addressing them:

PARENT-CHILD COMMUNICATION

Effective communication between parents and children is crucial for building strong relationships and addressing various issues that may arise. Here are some strategies for improving parent-child communication along with implementation examples:

1. Active Listening:

Implementation: When your child comes home from school and seems upset, sit down with them, maintain eye contact, and actively listen to what they have to say. Avoid interrupting or offering immediate solutions. Instead, say something like, "I'm here to listen. Tell me what's bothering you."

2. Open Dialogue:

Implementation: Create a routine of open dialogue by having family meals together. During these meals, encourage your child to talk about their day, share their thoughts, and discuss any concerns. For instance, ask questions like, "What was the best part of your day?" or "Is there anything on your mind you'd like to talk about?"

3. Setting Clear Expectations:

Implementation: Sit down with your child and discuss family rules and expectations. Be clear about what is expected in terms of chores, homework, and behaviour. Write down these expectations and have your child sign or agree to them. This provides a sense of clarity and responsibility.

4. Empathy and Understanding:

Implementation: When your child faces a challenge, acknowledge their feelings and provide emotional support. For instance, if your child is upset about receiving a low grade, say, "I understand you're feeling disappointed. It's okay to feel that way. Let's talk about how we can work on improving your grades."

5. Problem-Solving Together:

Implementation: Involve your child in solving problems within the family. If there's a conflict about screen time, gather as a family to discuss the issue. Ask your child for their input on setting reasonable screen time limits, and work together to come up with a plan that everyone can agree on.

6. Respect for Individuality:

Implementation: Recognize and respect your child's individuality. If your child has a unique interest or hobby, show interest and support. For instance, if your child is passionate about painting, encourage them by setting up an art corner in the house and displaying their artwork.

7. Quality Time:

Implementation: Dedicate a time daily to connect with your child. Most times this looks impossible because it's not something on your radar and you are not held accountable for it. This is why we created the connection tool system in the inner circle problem where every parent gets content to deliver as they spend time with their children. The inner circle system also brings this to your consciousness daily, it's not about how much time you spend but what happens in that time. I have come to realise that the problem in parenting is not just quality time but what we do with that time and the content we bring in. Schedule one-on-one quality time with each child. This can be a special outing, a game night, or even reading a book together. This dedicated time allows for bonding and ensures that each child feels valued and heard.

8. Encourage Independence:

Implementation: As your child grows, encourage them to make age-appropriate decisions and take on responsibilities. You will need a road map for this and I shared about it in my book RAISING AN INDEPENDENT THINKING CHILD. If they're old enough to pack their lunch, allow them to do so, and praise their efforts even if it's not perfect.

9. Constructive Feedback:
Implementation: When offering feedback, focus on constructive criticism rather than criticism that may hurt their self-esteem. Instead of saying, "You're not good at math," you can say, "I see you're struggling with math. Let's work on it together."

10. Be a Role Model:
Implementation: Demonstrate the behaviours you want to see in your child. If you want them to be polite and respectful, model these behaviours in your interactions with them and others.

Effective parent-child communication involves patience, active listening, and mutual respect. By implementing these strategies, you can create an environment where your child feels comfortable expressing themselves, and where you can address issues and concerns together in a constructive and nurturing way.

SIBLING RIVALRY

Sibling rivalry is a common issue in many families, but it can be effectively addressed through open and effective communication. I wrote a book on "RESOLVING SIBLING RIVALRY" and shared how you can create systems that can help you resolve rivalry instead of overlooking it. Here's a step-by-step guide on how to solve sibling rivalry using communication:

1. Acknowledge the Issue:
Start by acknowledging that sibling rivalry is a normal part of growing up. Avoid denying or minimizing the problem; instead, recognize it as an opportunity for growth and learning.

2. Create a Safe Space for Communication:

Foster an environment where your children feel comfortable expressing their feelings. Ensure that they know they won't be judged or punished for sharing their emotions and concerns.

3. Active Listening:
Encourage your children to actively listen to each other when they have conflicts. Ensure that each child gets a chance to express their perspective without interruption. Teach them to reflect on what they've heard to ensure understanding.

4. Open Family Discussions:
Schedule regular family discussions to address sibling issues. Create a structured and safe space where everyone can express themselves. During these discussions, enforce rules of respectful communication.

5. Use "I Statements":
Teach your children to use "I statement" to express their feelings and concerns without blaming or accusing their siblings. For example, instead of saying, "You always take my things," they can say, "I feel upset when my things are borrowed without asking."

6. Identify Triggers and Patterns:
Help your children identify the triggers and patterns that lead to conflicts. Are there certain situations, times of day, or specific issues that frequently result in rivalry? Identifying these triggers can help in finding proactive solutions.

7. Problem-Solving Together:
Encourage your children to work together to find solutions to their conflicts. Ask them to brainstorm ideas for resolving specific issues. This approach promotes a sense of ownership and responsibility.

8. Set Clear Expectations:
Clearly define the family rules and expectations regarding respectful behaviour, sharing, and conflict resolution. Make sure that everyone understands the consequences of violating these rules.

9. Empathy and Understanding:

Promote empathy by encouraging your children to see things from their siblings' perspectives. This helps in understanding their feelings and needs. Encourage statements like, "How do you think your brother/sister feels right now?"

10. Celebrate Sibling Bonds:

Highlight the importance of sibling relationships and the positive aspects of having a brother or sister. Share stories and examples of moments when your children got along, played well together, or supported each other.

11. Be Consistent:

Consistency in enforcing the rules and expectations is crucial. Make sure that consequences for unacceptable behaviour are consistently applied.

12. Seek Professional Help If Needed:

If sibling rivalry is causing significant distress or escalating to harmful levels, consider seeking professional help from a family therapist or counsellor who specializes in family dynamics and conflict resolution.

Solving sibling rivalry through communication is an ongoing process that requires patience and consistency. By teaching your children effective communication and conflict-resolution skills, you can help them build stronger bonds and minimize rivalry, ultimately creating a more harmonious family environment.

FINANCES

Financial issues within a family can lead to stress and conflicts, but they can be effectively resolved through open and effective communication. Here's a step-by-step guide on how to address financial problems within your family using communication:

1. Start the Conversation:
Initiate an open and honest conversation about financial matters within the family. Find an appropriate time and place to sit down and discuss the issues.

2. Active Listening:
Encourage all family members to actively listen to each other. Ensure that each person has a chance to express their concerns and viewpoints. Avoid interrupting or being judgmental.

3. Share Financial Information:
Transparency is key. Share relevant financial information, such as income, expenses, debts, and savings. This helps everyone understand the family's financial situation.

4. Set Common Goals:
Identify common financial goals for the family, such as saving for education, a home, or a vacation. Discuss and prioritize these goals together.

5. Budgeting and Planning:
Create a family budget that outlines income, expenses, and savings. Allow family members to contribute their input into the budgeting process.

6. Define Financial Roles:
Clearly define the financial roles and responsibilities of each family member. This includes contributions to bills, savings, and discretionary spending.

7. Emergency Fund:
Discuss the importance of having an emergency fund and establish one as a family. Decide on how much to save and how it will be funded.

8. Debt Management:

If the family has debt, discuss a plan for managing and reducing it. Prioritize paying off high-interest debts to reduce financial stress.

9. Conflict Resolution:

Address any financial conflicts or disagreements that arise during the discussion. Encourage family members to work together to find solutions.

10. Seek Professional Help If Needed:

If financial problems are complex or cause significant stress, consider seeking assistance from a financial advisor or counsellor. They can provide guidance and expertise in managing financial issues.

11. Regular Financial Check-Ins:

Schedule regular family meetings to review the family's financial status and progress toward financial goals. This keeps everyone informed and accountable.

12. Be Supportive:

Encourage a supportive and understanding environment. If a family member is facing financial difficulties, offer emotional support and work together on solutions.

13. Financial Education:

Promote financial literacy within the family. Educate family members about budgeting, savings, investments, and other financial topics. This empowers everyone to make informed decisions.

14. Celebrate Achievements:

Celebrate financial achievements and milestones as a family. This can include reaching savings goals, paying off debts, or achieving financial stability.

Solving financial issues through communication is about involving all family members in the financial decision-making process. It encourages transparency, shared responsibility, and accountability. By fostering open discussions and collaborative problem-solving, families can alleviate financial stress, work toward common financial goals, and maintain a healthy financial outlook.

DIVORCE AND SEPARATION

Divorce or separation can be an emotionally challenging experience for families, but effective communication is key to managing the transition and ensuring the well-being of all family members. Here's a step-by-step guide on how to address divorce or separation issues within the family using communication:

1. Initiate Open Discussions:
Start the conversation about the divorce or separation by explaining the decision and its implications. Choose an appropriate time and place for this initial discussion.

2. Active Listening:
Encourage all family members to actively listen to one another's thoughts and feelings. Provide a space where everyone can express their concerns and emotions without interruption.

3. Be Honest and Age-Appropriate:
Tailor your communication to the age and maturity of each family member. Be honest but age-appropriate in your explanations. Avoid blame and judgment.

4. Answer Questions:
Be prepared to answer questions and address concerns. Children, in particular, may have many questions about the changes. Provide honest, simple answers without going into excessive detail.

5. Reassure Love and Support:
Reiterate your love and support for each family member. Ensure that they understand that your love for them remains unchanged, even if the family structure is changing.

6. Child-Centered Approach:
Adopt a child-centred approach, focusing on the well-being of the children. Emphasize that the decision is not their fault and that both parents will continue to be there for them.

7. Create a Co-Parenting Plan:

Work together with the other parent to create a co-parenting plan. This plan should address custody, visitation, and parental responsibilities. Keep communication open and respectful with the other parent.

8. Seek Professional Support:

Encourage family members to seek professional support, such as counselling or therapy, to cope with the emotional challenges of divorce or separation. Family therapy can also be beneficial to facilitate communication.

9. Consistency and Routine:

Maintain a sense of consistency and routine in the children's lives. This helps provide stability during the transition.

10. Age-Appropriate Discussions:

Initiate separate discussions with each child if they have different needs based on their age and understanding of the situation. Offer support tailored to their needs.

11. Be Patient:

Understand that family members may need time to process the changes. Be patient with their emotions and reactions, and be available to continue the conversation as needed.

12. Encourage Children's Expression:

Let children express their feelings through various means, such as writing, drawing, or talking. Encourage them to share their emotions and concerns.

13. Revisit and Adjust:

Periodically revisit the topic as family members adjust to the new situation. Continue to provide opportunities for open communication and check in on everyone's emotional well-being.

14. Avoid Negative Talk:

Refrain from negative talk about the other parent in front of the children. Encourage respectful communication and cooperation between both parents.

15. Celebrate Milestones:

Celebrate positive milestones and achievements within the family. This can include important events, personal accomplishments, and moments of bonding.

Effective communication during divorce or separation is about maintaining a supportive and child-centred approach. By fostering open, honest, and respectful conversations, families can help everyone navigate the transition with understanding and care, promoting emotional well-being during this challenging time.

SUBSTANCE ABUSE ISSUES

Dealing with substance abuse issues in the family can be emotionally challenging, but effective communication is essential for understanding the problem, offering support, and seeking solutions. I will recommend a lot of support from family members even at therapy. Here's a step-by-step guide on how to address substance abuse issues within the family using communication:

1. Initiate a Caring Conversation:

Start by initiating a private and non-confrontational conversation with the family member who may be struggling with substance abuse. Express your concern and genuine care for their well-being.

2. Active Listening:

Listen actively and attentively to their perspective and experiences. Avoid judgment or blame during this conversation. Let them share their feelings and thoughts without interruption.

3. Express Concerns and Feelings:

Share your feelings about the impact of substance abuse on the family. Use "I statements" to express how their actions affect you and your family. For example, say, "I feel worried and scared when I see you using substances."

4. Offer Support:

Reiterate your love and support for them. Make it clear that you intend to help, not to criticize. Offer your assistance in seeking help, whether it's through therapy, counselling, or support groups.

5. Avoid Enabling Behavior:

Communicate the need to avoid enabling substance abuse. This includes not covering up for them, not providing money for substances, and not minimizing the consequences of their actions.

6. Encourage Professional Help:

Recommend seeking professional help. Encourage them to speak with a therapist, counsellor, or addiction specialist who can provide the necessary guidance and treatment options.

7. Explore Treatment Options:

Collaborate with the family member to explore and discuss various treatment options, such as outpatient therapy, inpatient rehabilitation, or support groups. Be willing to participate in the process.

8. Family Therapy:

Consider family therapy to address the impact of substance abuse on family dynamics. Family therapy can help family members understand the situation, learn coping strategies, and work together to support recovery.

9. Maintain Boundaries:

Set and communicate clear boundaries regarding substance use within the family. Explain the consequences of violating these boundaries and be consistent in enforcing them.

10. Encourage Accountability:

Promote accountability for actions and choices. Encourage the family members to take responsibility for their behaviour and its impact on the family.

11. Celebrate Progress:

Celebrate small victories and progress made in the journey to recovery. Acknowledge and appreciate efforts to overcome substance abuse.

12. Educate Yourself:

Educate yourself about substance abuse, addiction, and the recovery process. Knowledge can help you better understand what your family member is going through.

13. Avoid Stigmatization:

Encourage a non-judgmental and empathetic attitude. Avoid stigmatizing language or behaviour, as it can create further barriers to seeking help.

14. Monitor and Check-In:

Continuously monitor your family member's progress and well-being. Regularly check in on their status, challenges, and needs.

Effective communication is the foundation for supporting a family member with substance abuse issues. By maintaining open, compassionate, and solution-focused conversations, you can help guide them toward recovery and ultimately create a healthier family environment.

BLENDED FAMILIES CHALLENGES

Blended families consisting of parents, stepparents, and stepchildren, often face unique challenges. Effective communication is crucial for navigating these complexities and fostering positive relationships. Here's a step-by-step guide on how to address blended family challenges using communication:

1. Initiate Open and Honest Discussions:
Create an environment where all family members feel safe to express their thoughts and concerns. Encourage open and honest dialogue.

2. Active Listening:
Promote active listening among family members. Ensure that each person has the opportunity to speak without interruption and that they feel heard and understood.

3. Define Roles and Expectations:
Clarify roles and expectations within the family. Discuss responsibilities, roles, and routines to avoid misunderstandings and conflicts.

4. Address Jealousy and Rivalry:
If there are issues of jealousy or rivalry among step-siblings, create a platform for them to express their feelings and concerns. Encourage empathy and understanding.

5. Family Meetings:
Schedule regular family meetings to discuss important matters and foster cooperation. Ensure that everyone has a voice during these meetings, and make decisions collectively.

6. Support the Bonding Process:

Encourage bonding activities between stepparents and stepchildren. Foster opportunities for quality time together, such as outings, shared hobbies, and interests.

7. Respect Individual Identities:
Emphasize the importance of acknowledging and respecting each family member's individuality and uniqueness. Encourage celebrating differences.

8. Stepparent-Stepchild Relationships:
If there are issues between stepparents and stepchildren, promote open communication. Encourage both parties to express their feelings and concerns, working toward mutual understanding.

9. Co-Parenting with Ex-Spouses:
Maintain respectful and open communication with ex-spouses, especially regarding issues related to shared custody or parenting responsibilities. Ensure that decisions are made in the best interests of the children.

10. Family Traditions:
Create new family traditions and rituals that involve all family members. This helps to unite the family and build shared experiences.

11. Encourage Empathy:
Foster empathy by encouraging family members to see things from each other's perspectives. Teach them to consider how their actions affect others in the family.

12. Seek Professional Guidance:
If blended family challenges persist or become overwhelming, consider seeking the assistance of a family therapist or counsellor who specializes in addressing blended family dynamics.

13. Avoid Favoritism:

Be aware of and avoid showing favoritism, whether intentional or unintentional, toward biological or stepchildren. Treat all children fairly and equally.

14. Be Patient:
Understand that building a strong blended family takes time. Be patient with the adjustment process and allow individual family members to adapt at their own pace.

15. Celebrate Achievements:
Celebrate the successes and positive moments within the blended family. Recognize milestones and achievements, whether big or small.

Effective communication within a blended family is essential for building trust, understanding, and a sense of belonging. By addressing challenges openly and empathetically, you can create a harmonious environment where all family members feel valued and supported.

AGEING PARENTS CHALLENGES

Caring for ageing parents or managing elderly care can be a complex and emotional journey. Effective communication is key to addressing the challenges and ensuring the best care for elderly family members. Here's a step-by-step guide on how to use communication to address ageing parents or elderly care challenges:

1. Initiate Family Discussions:

Start by initiating family discussions about the needs and preferences of ageing parents. Involve all family members to ensure that decisions are made collectively.

2. Active Listening:
Encourage active listening during family discussions. Ensure that all family members have a chance to express their concerns, suggestions, and feelings.

3. Assess Elderly Parents' Needs:
Work together to assess the specific needs of your elderly parents. This may include medical care, assistance with daily tasks, or emotional support.

4. Open Dialogue with Elderly Parents:
Foster open communication with elderly parents about their wishes and expectations regarding their care. Respect their autonomy and choices whenever possible.

5. Set Clear Roles and Responsibilities:
Define the roles and responsibilities of each family member in providing care. This includes financial contributions, caregiving duties, and decision-making.

6. Seek External Support:
Explore external support options, such as in-home care, respite care, or assistance from social workers or geriatric care managers. Discuss these options openly with the family.

7. Advance Planning:
Plan for the long term by addressing issues like housing, healthcare, legal matters, and end-of-life preferences. Engage in these conversations well in advance to avoid making hasty decisions during crises.

8. Family Meetings:

Schedule regular family meetings to review the care plan and discuss any adjustments or concerns. Keep the lines of communication open and adapt as needed.

9. Encourage Aging Parents' Independence:
Encourage ageing parents to maintain their independence as much as possible. Balance their need for support with their desire to stay self-sufficient.

10. Celebrate Milestones and Memories:
Celebrate and reminisce about milestones and memories with ageing parents. Create opportunities for family bonding and storytelling.

11. Coordinate with Siblings and Family Members:
If you have siblings or other family members involved in caregiving, maintain open communication and cooperation. Avoid conflicts by clarifying responsibilities and expectations.

12. Seek Professional Guidance:
If challenges become overwhelming or complex, consider consulting a geriatric care manager or a family therapist experienced in elder care to provide guidance and support.

13. Address Dementia or Health Issues:
If your elderly parents have health issues like dementia, communicate openly with healthcare professionals, caregivers, and family members to provide the best care possible.

14. Be Patient and Compassionate:
Understand that caregiving can be emotionally draining. Be patient and compassionate with your ageing parents and yourself. Offer emotional support to family members who are involved in caregiving.

15. Legal and Financial Matters:

Discuss and establish a plan for managing legal and financial matters related to the care of ageing parents. This includes wills, power of attorney, and financial responsibilities.

Effective communication is essential in addressing the complexities of ageing parents or elderly care. By fostering open and collaborative discussions within the family, you can provide the best care possible, ensure that everyone's needs are met, and create a supportive environment for your ageing loved ones.

CREATING A FAMILY COMMUNICATION PLAN

STEP	DESCRIPTION	ACTIONS AND COMPONENTS
1	Set Clear objectives	Define the primary goals and outcomes you want to achieve through improved family communication.
2	Identify Communication Channels	Determine the various channels you will use for family communication, such as family meetings, one-on-one conversations, and digital tools.
3	Develop Communication Guidelines	Establish ground rules for communication, emphasizing respect, active listening, and empathy. Ensure family members understand and agree to these guidelines.

4	Encourage Sharing and Feedback	Promote open and honest sharing of thoughts and emotions. Encourage family members to provide constructive feedback and offer support to one another.
5	Prioritize Quality Time	Schedule regular family quality time for bonding, shared experiences, and building stronger connections.
6	Create a Conflict Resolution Plan	Develop a plan for resolving conflicts constructively. Teach family members conflict resolution skills and strategies.
7	Communication Tools and Resources	Identify tools and resources that can facilitate communication, such as agendas for family meetings, online calendars, or communication apps.
8	Roles and Responsibilities	Define roles and responsibilities for family members in the communication plan, ensuring that everyone contributes to its success.
9	Implementation and Commitment	Begin implementing the communication plan and ensure that all family members commit to following its guidelines and principles.
10	Regular Evaluation and Adaptation	Schedule regular assessments and evaluations to measure the plan's effectiveness. Be prepared to make adjustments based on feedback and changing family dynamics.

This table provides a structured overview of the steps involved in creating a family communication plan, along with the actions and components needed for each step. It serves as a guide for families looking to enhance their communication and build stronger connections.

CONCLUSION

Effective communication is the cornerstone of healthy and thriving family relationships. It serves as the glue that holds families together, fosters understanding, and resolves conflicts. When communication is open, respectful, and empathetic, family members feel valued, heard, and supported. It enables the sharing of emotions, thoughts, and experiences, leading to stronger bonds and a sense of belonging.

In contrast, poor communication marked by criticism, condemnation, or neglect can lead to breakdowns in family relationships. To harness the power of effective communication, families must prioritize open dialogue, active listening, and constructive feedback. By doing so, they can navigate challenges, celebrate achievements, and build a harmonious and resilient family unit.

Effective communication within the family creates an atmosphere where it's easier for everyone to express their thoughts, their feelings, no matter how advanced. People can contribute to resolving conflicts and disagreements and in fortifying your bonds, this is important. Parenting doesn't require perfection, parenting requires that you get trained. We must train ourselves to be better and not assume perfection because that's one of the things that kills many family dynamics. One of the things that you must understand today is that you need training, you must be trained. Train yourself, sit down and ask yourself do I communicate effectively. I urge you today to begin to put in the work and get into training. It is about training yourself. I've learned to do things better, you too can learn to do things better.

Many times you are raising your voice, but it's not the solution, have you ever heard that when you lack wisdom, you begin to make noise? You are yelling because you lack wisdom of what to do, and what to apply at the time where you're supposed to apply it.
Parenting today demands wisdom and wisdom comes from the content of your knowledge, if you do not know you cannot give wisdom. You need to constantly ask yourself, what knowledge do I have? Change is noiseless and as your children are changing daily, you don't even recognize that they are changing so you need to catch up with the pace at which they are learning.

If your family is struggling with any form of unresolved family problems and you have started the work of resolution using effective communication; I want you to remember, that healing within a family is a continuous and dynamic journey. It involves acknowledging and addressing existing issues, fostering resilience, and building a positive and supportive environment. The healing journey begins with the recognition of communication breakdowns, emotional distance, or other challenges. By creating a family communication plan, setting clear objectives, and following communication guidelines, families can pave the way for positive change. Measuring progress through assessments and goals helps ensure that the family is moving in the right direction. Building stronger connections involves quality time, emotional support, and conflict-resolution skills. Ultimately, the healing journey is about working together to create a healthier, happier, and more harmonious family life. It's a path of continuous growth, understanding, and love that strengthens the bonds within the family and creates a safe and nurturing space for all its members.

I am rooting for you.

BOOKS AUTHOURED BY WENDY OLOGE

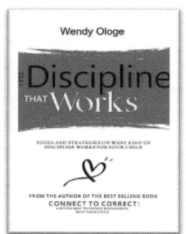

GUIDES AUTHORED BY WENDY OLOGE

1. Family media guide
2. Family value guide
3. Family meeting guide
4. Pre-Teen Skills Guide
5. Strong -willed child Flash cards
6. Discipline strategy Guide
7. Parent -Teacher Guide
8. Emotional Intelligent Guide
9. Sex Conversation Guide
10. The Learning Style Guide
11. Parenting Style Guide
12. Self Esteem Guide
13. Independent Thinking Guide
14. Structured Parenting Guide
15. Bully Prevention Toolkit
16. The ultimate Holiday Bundle
17. Back 2School Bundle
18. Amazing Christmas Bundle

NB: You can get these Books & Guides at our online store via

https://selar.co/m/TheIntentionalParentAcademy

Or on Amazon via amz.run/wendyologebooks

For more info:

Call:	08129687040
Learn more:	www.wendyologe.com
	www.theintentionalparentacademy.com
Email:	wendyologe@gmail.com

Printed in Great Britain
by Amazon

35881358R00079